PRACTICAL INTUITION

PRACTICAL INTUITION

How to Harness the Power of Your Instinct

and Make It Work for You

LAURA DAY

INTRODUCTION BY DEMI MOORE

VILLARD · NEW YORK

To my son, Samson, Shimshon,
named for the sun, which illuminates itself.
You shine brighter than your name.
Thank you.

FOREWORD
by Bruno del Rosso, M.D.

I first met Laura Day many years ago. When I was introduced to her, I was immediately struck by a palpable sensation. I actually felt this young woman to be the epicenter of some kind of radiant energy, the focal point of probing waves capable of penetrating any person or object they encountered. Her understanding seemed to sweep aside mysteries and pierce to the heart of things.

During my subsequent investigations of her ability in Rome (some of which are described later in this book), I collaborated with numerous researchers spanning diverse specialties. We performed numerous experiments, and in every session Laura never ceased to amaze and confound the assembled scientists and journalists. She obtained results greater than any of us had foreseen. It was as if the spirit of the world were gently mocking our understanding of nature through Laura's insights.

Laura takes readers of this book by the hand and helps them reconnect with a lost or forgotten part of themselves. It is my sincere hope that you will rediscover the hidden essence and profound workings of the way of the world. If you allow yourself the freedom to follow her guidance with an open mind, I am sure you will.

CONTENTS

AN INTRODUCTION
by Demi Moore

Do you believe in meaningful coincidences? One night I went to a party given by my friend Rosanna, and the minute I walked in the door she found me and said, "There's someone you have to meet. Trust me, you need to know her." Without hesitation, I took her hand, and she led me through the bubbling crowd. There, sitting at a table surrounded by an utterly captivated audience, was this tiny, waiflike woman with the most intense blue eyes. The intensity wasn't because of their color or shape, but because of the depth in which she looked at me; it seemed as if there were no limits to what she was seeing.

We had a lovely conversation except that, as she spoke, I realized we were talking about details and insights that only my closest friends could know about. Even more intriguing were the things she said that I share with absolutely no one. I became really curious, and asked what her profession was. She said she didn't like to say because she could never find a good name for it—but she assured me it was legal.

Our introduction was very brief, but in those few moments, I was completely struck by the calm sense of self she seemed to possess. That said, there couldn't have been a more perfect time in my life to meet someone like Laura Day. It was a time when I truly felt that anything and everything I could want was out there, waiting for me. I was newly married, expecting my first child, and in general, I felt invincible. My energy was skyrocketing with a limitless excitement, but I must confess it was a little all over the place and really needed some reining in.

At the end of that first encounter, she took my hand and said she wanted to remind me that I was exactly where I was supposed to be, and that all I needed was a little patience and everything else would fall in place. I knew immediately she was talking about my career. With the baby and the new marriage, my focus on my work had happily taken a backseat, and although it was certainly not my priority at this particular moment, my work was still very important to me. I think I had been worrying about it in the back of my mind, but not enough to make it an issue with anyone around me. Her parting words were of great comfort and insight, and reminded me to enjoy the ride.

The next time I had an opportunity to hook up with Laura was after my daughter was born and my career was slowly starting to pick up again. I'd just completed *Ghost* and had a few other films lined up. One in particular, *The Butcher's Wife*, required the consultation of a psychic for accuracy in the script, and once I understood what to refer to Laura's profession as, she was my first choice for the job. Paramount Pictures was thrilled to have her invaluable input on the film, and I seized the opportunity to better understand her gift myself.

During the course of making the movie, we spent many hours together working on notes to improve the character I was playing, as well as the film itself. At the end of one of the first sessions, Laura casually mentioned that if I wasn't quite ready to have another baby, I might want to be careful in the next few months. Well, I had to laugh, because at that moment my husband was shooting a film on the other side of the world in Rome. I said not to worry, but thanks for the warning. As time went by, she mentioned it once or twice more, then let it go, and back into the work we went. Every so often while we were working, she'd throw out a few personal pieces of information and I'd casually jot them down on my script. It was all very fascinating, but it didn't have much to do with what was going on at the moment, so I just chalked it up to a passing thought and moved on to the task at hand—making a movie.

Not thinking anything about what Laura had said months before, my husband returned for the last three weeks of my shoot, having completed his. Laura and I set up what was to be our last meeting on the script, and I had a very happy and passionate reunion with my husband. When I arrived for our last session, the first thing Laura asked me was "Are you pregnant?" As she watched the shocked smile creep on my face she said, "Congratulations!" She knew, and she knew. It turned out to be true.

When I first sat down to write this introduction to Laura's insightful book, I went rummaging around for some of the notes I had jotted down on that script of mine, looking for anything that would help me better explain my experiences with her intuitive ability. Well, to this day she never ceases to amaze me. In my scattered notes, I discovered that Laura had predicted not only the importance of a particular magazine cover having a profound effect on how people would perceive me, but that the major work of my career would not really begin until I hit my thirties—much to my dismay, I wrote then, considering I was only twenty-seven! Now, at thirty-three, I can see that what she said had come true: Some of the most important films of my career have occurred over the last few years. As I reflect over this recent time, including the ups and the downs, it absolutely feels like it's all just beginning—at least I hope so . . .

Laura Day is a remarkable woman with remarkable abilities, but for me, what is most remarkable about her is how she has taught me to believe in myself and my own intuition. Intuition is really nothing more than an internal mechanism that aids you in any and all of your decision-making. It's what some of us call a gut feeling, an instinct, a sense of something that tells you to go in one direction or another, and that, combined with training, gives you the tools to make solid decisions. The bigger question is not what intuition is or how it works, but whether or not we are willing to trust it and ourselves. I have survived on trusting my intuition and going with my instincts, but it is still so easy to allow a lot of external garbage to get in the way, to look for outside validation to reassure and comfort ourselves that we're doing the right thing, instead of going inward to find whatever answer we're seeking. As always, it is in the doing that we really make a difference in our lives, and the more I trusted my instincts and intuition, the more I started to believe in myself.

The problems come when we second-guess our intuition or fight against it, because it may be leading us in a direction we don't want to go. Then it becomes nothing more than a power struggle with ourselves. Which usually leads to a wonderful learning experience from having made a choice, not a bad choice, just a choice, but one that will no doubt be of greater struggle. Why do we torture ourselves like this? Mostly because we lack the tools and information, but even more because we allow fear and a lack of faith in ourselves to run our lives.

If there is one thing I can say about my own personal journey, it is that we are not meant to do it all alone. As I have sought answers, I have come to know a few wonderful people with gifts similar to Laura's, and just like her, they are teachers who want to use their gifts to be of service. As a woman and as a mother, I have seen Laura's commitment to educating people and releasing their fears. By creating a practical format like the one in this book, she can teach you how intuition works on all levels of our lives, and how we can take back our personal power . . . instead of giving it away. Enjoy the journey, and think of this book as nothing more than a map.

THE SEVEN STEPS TO INTUITIVE DEVELOPMENT

OPENING

NOTICING

PRETENDING

TRUSTING

REPORTING

INTERPRETING

INTEGRATING

PRACTICAL INTUITION

- 1 -

How I Became
an Intuitive

A Scientific Gathering

Lunch is over. Champagne glasses are refilled as the attendees wait for the demonstration to begin. The apartment's enormous living room is richly appointed with magnificent works of art and beautiful marble floors. The large windows reveal a vista of Rome's famous skyline on this overcast, early spring afternoon. She recognizes the Vatican and the Spanish Steps in the distance and then turns around to face the group.

She is tiny, almost waiflike, and even at age twenty-one could easily be mistaken for a French schoolgirl. Her blond hair falls to her shoulders. She is dressed in navy and white, her pale knees crossed beneath her pleated skirt. She sinks into the soft pillows of the enormous brocade couch; her blue, flat shoes don't even reach the floor.

She is nervous, never having appeared in front of a group before, and certainly not one so distinguished as this. Around her are several dozen formally attired psychologists, physicians, and other experts. Journalists are on hand to record the event.

She reviews the assortment of objects on the ornate table in front of her. She sees numerous sealed envelopes and identical small closed boxes containing various objects brought by the attendees. The envelopes and boxes are unmarked so that no one in the room knows which box or envelope contains his or her item.

Dr. del Rosso is seated beside her, holding her left hand reassuringly. She smiles. With his gray, pointed beard, he reminds her of Merlin the Magician.

Everyone takes a seat and settles in. The audience grows silent as Dr. del Rosso selects one of the closed boxes at random and hands it to her. She looks down at it for a moment, then stares off into the distance, as if gathering her thoughts. As she does so, Dr. del Rosso adjusts the microphone on the table and turns on the tape recorder.

"The twenty-first day of March nineteen eighty," he says in Italian. He adjusts the microphone in the young woman's direction and settles back in the couch. She begins.

"I see air moving in and out of little holes . . . making sounds."

She speaks slowly; Italian is not her native tongue. Though fluent, she pauses frequently to capture the nuances of her impressions. Journalists scribble away on their tiny reporter notebooks.

"Wood and metal. . . . The person was very sad when he bought this. . . . Going away somewhere he didn't . . . didn't want to go. . . . He is lonely, away from his family. It makes a pretty sound, though."

She stops, apparently finished. She hands the unopened box back to Dr. del Rosso.

"Whose box is this?" he asks the audience.

"Um, I think it's mine," responds Dr. Cosco tentatively, from the back of the room.

"Has she identified your object? Would you like to question her?"

"Signorina," Dr. Cosco says, "if you would, please open the box."

She does so and removes a wood and metal harmonica. She hands it to Dr. del Rosso, who holds it up for everyone to see. Many oohs and ahs as they recognize the accuracy of the young woman's intuitive description. Dr. Cosco explains the meaning the harmonica has for him: "I bought it when I was leaving for military duty. I got this when I was far away from home to keep me company. I carried it with me all through military service. I didn't want to go. I left so much behind. . . ." He becomes lost in reverie as Dr. del Rosso continues his demonstration.

"Hand her another box," he instructs his female assistant. She picks up an oblong box and offers it to the young woman everyone has come that afternoon to observe. This time, however, she shakes her head. Dr. del Rosso's assistant nods in agreement.

"I don't want to touch that box. I'm probably just imagining things, but it feels like a knife."

With a raised eyebrow, Dr. del Rosso directs his assistant to open the box. She draws out a letter opener shaped like a knife. More oohs and ahs and much stroking of gray beards and knowing nods of heads from the distinguished doctors.

"Who has brought a photograph?"

An ancient professor holds up a sealed envelope and steps forward. He hands it to the assistant, who in turn hands it to the young woman. By this time she has removed her shoes and pulled up her knees, shifting on the couch to find a more comfortable position. Before she begins to speak, another professor interrupts her.

"How do you do this?" he asks, somewhat anxiously.

"I don't know."

Almost before she has finished speaking, the interrogator volunteers a complicated, scientific-sounding hypothesis of her ability, which he attributes to the stress of early childhood trauma. Dr. del Rosso cuts short his "explanation."

"Please."

Everyone is rapt with attention as the young woman begins to speak.

"This is a woman. In the picture she is young, but I think she is quite old now. . . . I hear French. There is a great deal of iron in the house; someone works with iron. . . . I also see many paintings around the woman, but I smell iron."

Dr. del Rosso asks the audience whether they would like to question her. Dr. Pucci steps forward.

"Does she live alone? Is she married?"

"Yes, she's married. . . . No, maybe not. No. She lives with a man, but it doesn't feel like . . . they . . ."

She looks away, embarrassed. She wants to say that she does not feel the man and woman are sexually involved but does not know how to express this delicately.

"Perhaps a relative. . . . He is older . . . maybe now he isn't alive. She is an artist. It's the man who works with iron. . . . No, they are not married. She never married. . . . Now she lives alone. Her back hurts, makes her walk funny. . . . She's old now. I want to see her."

The young woman starts to open the envelope, but Dr. del Rosso interrupts her. "Wait, perhaps Professor Pucci has some more questions."

"No. I want to see her now," she declares, surprisingly assertive for someone so demure. She opens the envelope to reveal the faded picture of a beautiful young girl.

Dr. Pucci addresses the audience: "This is a picture of my sister. Yes, please hold up the picture, Signorina. Thank you. Of course, this was taken quite some time ago, when we were much younger. My father earned his trade working with iron until he fell ill. My sister cared for him until he died in our family home."

"But the French, she said she heard French," shouts someone.

"Our family home is in the south of France," Dr. Pucci says. "My sister was an artist; never married."

The young woman is touched. She looks down at the photograph. "She was so pretty," she says to herself. "Sad. I like this woman."

Dr. del Rosso addresses the assembled guests, referring to the young woman next to him. "This subject exhibits one of the most acute abilities of extrasensory perception I have ever seen. She cannot, of course, explain this ability, as it is something she has apparently never been without, and, not being a scientist, she is unable to analyze this ability. Dr. Lagambina and I have some theories as to why she developed in this way. Some of the developmental aspects are apparent, although we haven't investigated either the psychological or physiological possibilities that may indicate a function—or dysfunction, if you prefer—of this type of . . ."

The young woman seems not to hear as she holds the tattered old photograph wistfully, thinking of Dr. Pucci's dark-haired sister.

Fifteen years have passed since that afternoon, but I remember it as if it were yesterday. As you may have guessed, I was the young woman on the couch. I've been tested on many other occasions, and since that time I've developed a career as a practicing intuitive (a word I prefer to *psychic*, the more popular but misleadingly esoteric expression).

I wrote this book to show you how you, too, can develop an ability I've used since childhood.

DISCOVERING A TALENT

I am frequently asked how I learned to be an intuitive. The question is like asking a one-legged man how he learned to hop. If you lose a leg, you're forced to develop and use the other.

In my case the limb I lacked was the information and skill to cope with a prematurely adult role that I was assigned by family difficulties. As is the case with any child, I didn't have the emotional and intellectual ability to perform as an adult. My intuitive abilities flourished by way of compensation. I developed my intuition as a survival response, and it has served me well.

I cannot recall a time when I didn't receive strong intuitive impressions. When I was twelve years old, my mother fell into a coma from which she was not expected to recover. Nonetheless, I received the feeling that she was going to survive. Although I hadn't been told the specifics of her condition, I had a clear sense of what was not working in her body.

Each day when I went to the hospital, I felt an instinctive need to breathe in a certain way until my body got very warm. In my mind's eye I could see the parts of her body that needed healing, and I would send this warmth—this energy—to them.

After two weeks, my mother emerged from the coma and went on to make a full physical recovery. She told me that during the time she was in the coma, she could feel me pulling her back. Over the years I became braver in giving the information I received for people in need, and, although I certainly never "decided" to make it a career, I had time for little else, so it evolved into one.

As is so often the case with children, I didn't realize until I was in my teens that everyone did not perceive things exactly the way I did. I discovered that if I said all the ideas that "came" to me when in conversation, the other person would think me strange at best and frightening at worst.

These abilities were certainly never encouraged by my family. I come from three generations of physicians. While my father respects that I believe in what I am doing and that I am making a contribution to the world in my own way, I'm sure he would have chosen a more traditional career for me.

As the saying goes, when the student is ready the teacher will appear. By my early teens I was "ready," and a number of teachers or mentors entered my life. I was fortunate to meet a variety of people from both spiritual and scientific communities who helped me realize that my perceptions were a useful and not so very uncommon ability, to be developed and used ethically and responsibly.

My grandmother told me that as a young woman she helped my grandfather do medical research in his laboratory. She did not know very much about medicine, so her job was mostly to clean up and be of use in other little ways. Yet every once in a while, when my grandfather was stuck with an experiment, the solution would come to her "from nowhere."

So apparently intuitive ability runs in my family. In my grand-mother's era, however, this ability was something to be kept secret. I am fortunate to be living at a time in which intuition is not only accepted but valued.

In my early twenties, I taught my first class in intuitive train-ing. What had been until then merely a useful ability suddenly became my "official" career. Now I will share with you everything I've learned over the past three decades about intuition and help you rediscover a talent you've always had.

- 2 -
What Intuition
Can Do for You

The End of an Age

As the end of the second millennium draws near, the limitations of logic, rationality, and the "scientific method" as the sole means of guiding our lives are becoming all too painfully clear. Increasingly our world is turning to modes of perception and understanding that don't rely on evidence presented to our senses, modes such as intuition and faith.

The overreliance on "linear" thought that characterizes the modern era is a relatively recent phenomenon in human history. Perhaps its greatest exponent was the great French Enlightenment philosopher René Descartes. Descartes carried on an intellectual tradition whose roots go back to ancient Greece. But remember, ancient Greece—the birthplace of logic, philosophy, and the rudiments of the scientific method—was also the land of the Delphic Oracle. The early Greeks recognized that rational thought is incomplete and needs the support of intuition. By the end of this book, you'll see that the intuitive method can be at least as rigorous as the "scientific" one.

Intuition Rediscovered

Intuition has a dubious reputation in these times. Conventional wisdom dismisses it as something intangible, mystical, unreliable—and hence the province of women. Men, to the extent that they're allowed to be intuitive at all, have "hunches" or "gut responses" or "instincts."

These are myths and misconceptions. Women are *not* more intuitive than men. Perhaps because intuition was thought not to be a rational process it was attributed to women, whereas rational thought was assumed to be the province of male brains. In fact, tasks or jobs traditionally assumed to be "women's work" required very little in the way of intuition.

I wrote this book to show you that men and women are equally intuitive and equally equipped to use this powerful tool in their everyday lives.

HOW I USE INTUITION

I have been a practicing intuitive in the United States and Europe for almost two decades. My intuitive abilities have been verified in studies by university professors on two continents. An intuitive, by the way, is simply someone who consciously uses intuition in his or her daily or professional life. I say "consciously" uses intuition because, as you will see shortly, you *unconsciously* use it all the time.

Although intuition has an ethereal connotation, let me assure you that it can be used in highly practical ways. With practice, which this book will provide, it can be used to deliver precise, tangible, reliable—in a word, *useful*—information.

How useful? The people who consult me are highly practical men and women. I've worked with doctors, lawyers, CEOs, politicians, and investors, as well as actors and celebrities whose names you'd recognize.

I've used intuition in every conceivable practical application:

· to find lost people in locations I had never seen
· to analyze stock offerings and to forecast the price of gold and the Dow Jones average six months ahead
· to diagnose illnesses that have puzzled doctors and to predict the effectiveness of new drugs

· to develop courtroom strategies and to anticipate the questions of opposing attorneys
· and for fun and profit, to bet on horses

So can you.

You may be wondering how it's possible for me to be an expert in so many areas. In fact, with the exception of medical science, I know next to nothing about these fields. As you will discover shortly, the *less* you know about a subject or topic, the more effectively your intuition comes into play!

AN INVESTOR PLACES BILLION-DOLLAR BETS ON HIS INTUITION

George Soros is arguably the greatest investor of all time. If you had been lucky enough to invest money with him twenty-five years ago, you would have seen it double every two or three years! Soros has the distinction of earning more as an investor in one year ($650 million) than anyone else in history. To do that, he routinely takes positions of a billion dollars or more.

If you ask professors of finance at any business school whether a person can consistently beat the market averages, they will say it's mathematically and scientifically impossible. Perhaps, if you base your investment decisions solely on mathematics and science. Soros, in a revealing comment, suggests that he does not.

In his recent book *Soros on Soros,* he was asked whether he used a formal (i.e., quantitative, scientific, objective) procedure to cut losses when his position moved against him and how he found out when things (i.e., his logic) were "going wrong." Here's how he responded:

> I feel the pain. *I rely a great deal on animal instincts.* When I was actively running the Fund, I suffered from backache. I used the onset of acute pain as a signal that there was something wrong in my portfolio. The backache didn't tell me what was wrong—you know, lower back for short positions, left shoulder for currencies—but it did prompt me to look for something amiss when I might not have done so otherwise. That is not the most scientific way to run a portfolio. [emphasis added]

It may not be a scientific way to run a portfolio, but there is no arguing with Soros's incredible successes. I do not mean to suggest that you should withdraw your money from your mutual fund if you wake up with a backache tomorrow morning. Keep in mind that Soros is an astute thinker who deeply analyzes the economic, political, and psychological climate before making an investment. What is fascinating is that he relies on his intuition to tell him when his logic is incorrect.

You can learn to do the same.

WHY I WROTE THIS BOOK

My goal is not to turn you into a practicing intuitive. Rather, I want to show you how to use intuition in your daily professional as well as personal life. The part of my work I enjoy the most is teaching people to rediscover and develop their natural intuitive abilities.

I'll show you how you can use intuition to enhance every area of your daily life. I'll show you how to use it to recover lost information about the past, verify unknown information about the present, or predict information about the future.

Intuition can empower you to be productive and active in any situation. As the world becomes increasingly specialized, it's more and more difficult to remain an informed participant. We hand over decisions to experts and specialists who "know better," like doctors, lawyers, automobile mechanics, or insurance agents.

With intuition you'll be able to reclaim some measure of competence and control over these areas of your life. I'll show you how you can gain practical information about anything, whether it's a medical condition you know nothing about or the breakdown of a machine whose interior is inaccessible.

Most of all, intuition will improve your decision making. I'll show you how to combine your intuitions with your feelings and judgments to enhance your powers of decision immeasurably.

Intuition should be an integral part of your life, like exercise or meditation. Employing it will open you up and add to the quality of both your thinking and your emotional selves.

THIS IS A PRACTICAL BOOK

This is not a spiritual or esoteric book about the mystical uses of intuition. Nor is it a theoretical book for philosophers or psychologists or others with a merely academic interest in this topic (though I expect they will find the implications of my themes highly thought provoking).

Does intuition work? Yes! How it works I still can't be sure, though I'll offer some speculations later. Fortunately, we don't need to know how intuition works to use it.

No, this is a book about using your intuitive sense to answer the nuts-and-bolts questions of your daily life. This book provides everything you need to develop your intuitive potential to its fullest. And I'll hold your hand each step of the way.

PRACTICE MAKES PERFECT

You develop your intuition by applying it consciously through practice, not by reading about it. Reading is primarily an intellectual act, and your thinking mind can interfere with your intuitive mind.

You'll need to do some exercises, the same ones I've been using in my workshops for nearly twenty years. I know they work, and besides, they're fun to do.

To give you models with which you can compare your work, I've also provided examples from typical students. I've made a point of selecting *typical* responses, "mistakes" and all.

WHAT YOU'LL NEED

To get the most from the intuitive exercises in this book, a tape recorder is very helpful. It's best to practice using your intuition as you will be using it in real life. Generally that means speaking out loud rather than writing, so a recorder can take down your responses for later transcription.

Another advantage to speaking out loud is that doing so gives your reflective mind less time to interfere in the intuitive process.

You can write the exercises down, but, since it's better to speak continuously, most people have trouble writing fast enough to keep up with the flow of their intuitive impressions. In fact, being able to keep up with your impressions is a good sign that they are not intuitive.

Since you'll be working through numerous exercises in the coming chapters, a loose-leaf notebook would be helpful. Be sure to use a new page for each exercise so you can easily compare your work on different exercises. Get one that has pockets to keep the scraps of your work in one place. Once you have tape-recorded your responses, you can transcribe them in written form in your notebook.

HOW THIS BOOK IS ORGANIZED

Most chapters in this book are brief and intended as complete "experiences." Throughout the text, I have interspersed exercises. I've presented these exercises in sequential fashion, each one laying the groundwork for the next. Don't skip around. Begin at the beginning and read straight through.

YOU MAY NOT ALWAYS UNDERSTAND WHAT I'M ASKING YOU TO DO

Occasionally I'll ask you to do an exercise whose point will not be revealed until several chapters later. Some students find this frustrating, but it's all part of the learning process. Trust that if you're doing the exercises conscientiously, you are getting from them what you should—even if you don't understand what you're being asked to do.

IF YOU PREFER, IGNORE EVERYTHING I HAVE TO SAY

Again, this is a practical book. The only way to develop your intuition is to use it. The chapter texts tell you about intuition to satisfy your curiosity and to answer common questions. It's quite possible, however, to develop your intuitive powers without understanding what you're doing or why. I am not being facetious, then, when I say that (if you're short of time and need to skim this book) you can skip the text and confine your attention to the exercises.

TAKE YOUR TIME

Using this book for your intuition is like going to a gym for your mind. As you do the exercises, you will enlarge your capacity for using intuition in practical ways. Each exercise is targeted to a different intuitive capacity, such as noticing or reporting or integrating. In essence, you're teaching your unconscious to provide the many parts that make up a "reading" in a way your conscious mind can use.

Try not to read this book in one sitting. Rediscovering and developing your intuition will not happen overnight. Indeed, many of the exercises while simple should be practiced daily.

DON'T PEEK AT THE ANSWERS!

The numerous exercises throughout this book are keyed to answers that are given at the bottom of nearby pages. When checking your work on a particular exercise, try not to let your eyes wander. Even a momentary glance is enough for your subconscious to record information we want your intuition to discover.

REMEMBER TO TAKE CARE OF YOURSELF

Over the coming days and weeks, you will be working very hard and exercising parts of yourself that you may not be used to touching. Your mind and body will need all the rest and care you can get.

Shift your focus as much as possible to things that ground you. Eat good meals. Take walks. Exercise. Stretch. Get a massage.

OK then, let's get started. Since this book is about helping you develop and use intuition in *your* life, in the next chapter I'll ask you to get in touch with your goals, values, and priorities.

- 3 -

ESTABLISHING WHAT IS
TRULY IMPORTANT TO YOU

WHAT ARE YOU ALL ABOUT?

It has been said that each individual's life boils down to a single question. Your life is the living of that question, the search for its answer and personal significance. Arriving at that ultimate question involves asking and answering numerous preliminary questions. Slowly, you begin to realize all the questions' interrelatedness, until at last you distill them down to one. You do this not by gaining information from empirical sources but by questioning yourself and unearthing knowledge you didn't know you possessed.

This answering of a question with a question that reveals a still greater truth is a fundamental part of many religious traditions, including Hebraic, Jesuitical, and Zen. It's in reaching the profound, seminal questions that the meaning is discovered and the questioning taken to the next level of understanding. The questions lead us to places unfamiliar and then make these places known to us.

An insightful psychotherapist once said to me, "You want answers to questions that only you could think to ask." At the time I thought he was validating my intellectual superiority. But I've come to realize that certain questions are so intricately tied to our individuality that the answers can come only from within ourselves. Often this is the last place we look.

The function of intuition is to lead us to these answers. The function of the mind and the heart is to formulate the questions.

This book will help you answer your questions by asking them back at you. Indeed, only you can answer the ultimate questions of your life. It always amazes me that we expect disciplines like philosophy and religion and intuition to answer questions such as What is the meaning of life? Yet we don't think that the individual "I" who generates these philosophies can answer something simple like Will the price of gold rise in February? or Where the heck did I leave my car keys? or, more seriously, How can I make my relationship more successful?

It's the little questions that make up life.

≋

INTUITION IN ACTION
A STUDENT'S ANECDOTE

I am a medical doctor. I remember I was wolfing down some lunch between appointments. After lunch I was scheduled to see a new middle-aged female patient. As I munched on my sandwich, I sensed that something might be wrong with her thyroid gland. Remember, I had never seen her before. I made a mental note to do a complete thyroid workup on her, even though she had no complaints and was coming in for a routine annual examination. Indeed, she appeared completely healthy.

I performed a series of thyroid tests on her anyway. Several days later, the laboratory results reveal suspiciously low levels of the hormones thyroxine and calcitonin.

With this evidence, I called my patient back for a more detailed examination. Confirming my intuitive diagnosis, a radiologist subsequently discovered an almost imperceptible nodule on her thyroid that had escaped prior detection. I referred my patient to a specialist who treated her condition in time to prevent potentially dangerous complications.

This is just one of many instances that come to mind of incorporating intuition in my professional life since I have been trained in its use. I would never act solely on an intuitive "hit," but intuition rarely fails to provide promising "leads."

≋

GETTING IN TOUCH WITH YOUR PRIORITIES

The following is a simple questionnaire that will help you pinpoint the information you need to best use the next chapter. This is also your first exercise in opening the door to intuition.

≈

EXERCISE 1
GETTING IN TOUCH WITH YOURSELF

PART I

Record your *first* response to each of the following questions, even if it doesn't seem to make sense. Be honest. Don't try to be clever or to respond in a way you think will impress me or others. Be brief; sometimes a word will suffice. You will have the opportunity to give more reflective answers shortly.

Although this exercise calls for short responses, you may want to have a friend read off the questions and transcribe your answers. If not, use your tape recorder.

Remember, I want your *immediate* responses. OK? Here goes:

- In this moment, what do you want?
- In this moment, what do you need?
- In this moment, what is your greatest fear?
- In this moment, what is your dearest wish?
- In this moment, what do you need to be happy?
- In this moment, what is your ambition?
- In this moment, what is your greatest talent?
- In this moment, what is your most formidable obstacle?
- In this moment, how are you your own worst enemy?
- In this moment, with what part of your life are you most satisfied?
- In this moment, what is missing in your life?
- In this moment, in which area of your life would you most like to see change in the coming year?
- What is your mission?

PART II

Review your answers to the preceding questions. I would now like you to *reflect* on each question before responding. Your answers this time will be longer than those in Part I, but you should still try to be concise. If you get stuck, look back to your initial responses.

Here goes:

- Upon reflection, what do you want?
- Upon reflection, what do you need?
- Upon reflection, what is your greatest fear?
- Upon reflection, what is your dearest wish?
- Upon reflection, what do you need to be happy?
- Upon reflection, what is your ambition?
- Upon reflection, what is your greatest talent?
- Upon reflection, what is your most formidable obstacle?
- Upon reflection, how are you your own worst enemy?
- Upon reflection, with what part of your life are you most satisfied?
- Upon reflection, what is missing in your life?
- Upon reflection, in which area of your life would you most like to see change in the coming year?
- Upon reflection, what is your mission?

Record your responses in your intuition notebook. If you used a tape recorder, transcribe your precise words.

Remember to label this Exercise 1 and note the date.

≈≈≈

ONE STUDENT'S RESPONSES

The following transcription is a model of a typical student's responses. By way of background, I'll tell you that she is a young woman going through a difficult divorce. Again, the student examples I've selected are representative of someone—like you—beginning the process of intuitive development. I have consciously avoided using outstanding or precocious illustrations.

· In this moment, what do you want?
  "Home."
· In this moment, what do you need?
  "Help."
· In this moment, what is your greatest fear?
  "Obliteration."
· In this moment, what is your dearest wish?
  "Harmony."
· In this moment, what do you need to be happy?
  "Strength."
· In this moment, what is your ambition?
  "Love."
· In this moment, what is your greatest talent?
  "Love."
· In this moment, what is your most formidable obstacle?
  "Myself."
· In this moment, how are you your own worst enemy?
  "My fear."
· In this moment, with what part of your life are you most
  satisfied?
  "Love."
· In this moment, what is missing in your life?
  "Security."
· In this moment, in which area of your life would you most
  like to see change in the coming year?
  "Resolution."
· What is your mission?
  "To love."

Here are the student's responses when she reflected on the
questions:

· Upon reflection, what do you want?
  "To have a solid, balanced existence."
· Upon reflection, what do you need?
  "Money and clarity."
· Upon reflection, what is your greatest fear?
  "Having harm come to any of the persons dear to me."

- Upon reflection, what is your dearest wish?
  "To have a happy home life."
- Upon reflection, what do you need to be happy?
  "The clarity and resources available to protect and maintain those I love."
- Upon reflection, what is your ambition?
  "To have a happy family."
- Upon reflection, what is your greatest talent?
  "Creating beauty in the mundane."
- Upon reflection, what is your most formidable obstacle?
  "My lack of clarity and organization, and my emotionalism."
- Upon reflection, in what way are you your own worst enemy?
  "I am constantly doubting myself, instead of having faith in my choices and motivations."
- Upon reflection, with what part of your life are you most satisfied?
  "My relationship with my significant other, my career; who my child is as a person."
- Upon reflection, what is missing in your life?
  "Support, reliable support, someone to whom I can delegate concerns."
- Upon reflection, in which area of your life would you most like to see change in the coming year?
  "The positive resolution of my marital conflict."
- Upon reflection, what is your mission?
  "To create, to cocreate, harmony around me and within me."

THE POINT OF THIS EXERCISE

This is a book about answering the important questions in your life. You've just begun the process of thinking about them. In the next chapter, I'll ask you to think about them more concretely.

≈

INTUITION IN ACTION
A STUDENT'S ANECDOTE

My friend Anne was troubled by a phone call she had recently received. Matthew, her four-year-old son, had displayed highly aggressive outbursts at his preschool. The teachers and even some of the other parents had begun to complain. Anne and her husband had racked their brains unsuccessfully to uncover the cause of their child's problem.

So she called me discuss her problem. Not having seen Anne's son for over a year, I pictured an old grandfather in her mind. I felt that was the little boy's fear. I became aware that Matthew is afraid everyone around him will become ill as his grandfather recently did.

I told Anne my impressions. She confirmed that her father had recently suffered a stroke and that Matthew had been distressed to see him bedridden.

I told Anne that I sensed the way Matthew defended himself against his fears was to immerse himself in whatever he was doing. Efforts to break his concentration, however friendly, were likely to be viewed by him as aggression. So, for example, if a teacher were to speak with Matthew while he was absorbed in painting a picture, Matthew might scream at her to go away.

As I told Anne about her son's difficulties, I got more in touch with my intuitive state. I became clearer and more detailed in my description. Anne later told me that everything I had been saying seemed almost to come from her son's lips.

With this new understanding of the problem, Anne and her husband set up a teacher-parent conference. They informed Matthew's teacher of what was troubling him. Together they worked to find ways to help Matthew express himself and tried to give him tools to integrate interruptions of his concentration safely.

≈

- 4 -

GRANTING YOU
THREE WISHES

JUST IMAGINE, YOU CAN ASK ANYTHING . . .

I'd like you to imagine that you're about to be granted a special audience with an all-seeing individual. It's hard to believe, but this person can tell you anything you want to know about any person or event in the past, present, or even future.

Now, just like Aladdin's genie, this omniscient being has granted you a wonderful gift: the answers to any three questions of your choosing. Any three. What questions would you ask?

They wouldn't be trivial—you have been granted just three, after all. This would *not* be the appropriate time to focus on where you left your car keys or whether you should substitute chestnuts for walnuts in your mother's Thanksgiving recipe for turkey stuffing. You wouldn't want to waste this once-in-a-lifetime opportunity.

No, these questions would involve major life issues. Very likely they would concern your career or your relationships. Your questions might be about obstacles or opportunities you're likely to encounter in the coming months and how best to deal with them. Or perhaps there is a mystery from your past you'd like to solve once and for all.

Since you'll want to be able to use the information, you wouldn't ask about events decades from now. You'd ask about issues you could verify one way or another in the next six to twelve months, a few years at the outside. If you asked about the meaning of life, for example, you would not ever be able to verify whether the answer you were given was correct.

$$\approx\approx$$

EXERCISE 2
SO, WHAT WOULD YOU ASK?

Right now, get a pen and a piece of paper and come up with three questions. They can be about personal or business matters. They can be about yourself, someone you know, or someone who hasn't even come into your life yet.

Three questions.

Don't be shy, really let loose. No one is going to see these questions but you. Don't think any of your questions are silly. "Will my breasts ever grow?" would have been my main question in the years between childhood and adolescence!

These need not be yes/no questions. They should be varied and not overlapping, though they don't have to be in any particular order.

Again, ask questions you really want answered.

Don't worry about whether you've phrased your questions perfectly. In the next chapter you will be editing them.

If you have trouble narrowing your wish list down to three, brainstorm with as many questions as you'd like. Once you've completed your longer list, use process of elimination to select the three questions you would *most* like answers to.

When you've finished writing them, label the list Exercise 2 and place it in your intuition notebook.

$$\approx\approx$$

HERE'S MY PROMISE

By the time you've finished this book, you will have detailed answers to your three questions. You don't need to do research, ask an expert, or call the Psychic Hot Line (a psychic 900 number).

How, you ask? Well, do you remember that person I mentioned whom you can consult, that remarkable individual with access to answers about any question?

I was talking about *you*.

As you will discover shortly, you are already intuitive. You access your "sixth sense" unconsciously all the time. You simply aren't aware of your intuition, or haven't learned to recognize it. Trust me: You have the ability—right now—to get useful information instantly on any topic at any time, whether intellectually you know anything about it or not.

This book will help you develop your conscious control over this amazing faculty. Through the exercises you will answer each question not just once but over and over, from different perspectives and in different time frames. Incidentally, there is nothing preventing you from answering other questions on your own as you hone your intuitive ability. The limit to three is simply so I can walk you through the exercises in an organized way. I know this program works because over the past decade I've helped thousands of people tap their intuition. By the end of this book, you'll be using your intuitive powers like never before.

Remember, I'm not going to answer your three questions. You are.

That means you'll have to complete the exercises conscientiously. Since they're all about the major questions in your life, I'm sure they'll have your complete attention. Besides, they're brief and fun, and they'll give you instant feedback on your progress.

IF YOU HAVE ANY DOUBTS

You may be skeptical that anyone, much less you, can answer these questions. I don't blame you. Many of my students begin as skeptics.

So I'm going to ask you to do something I ask of them. If you don't believe you can answer these questions, I'd like you to cultivate an attitude you may have forgotten since childhood. I'd like you *to pretend*.

Your ability to pretend is such an important part of your intuitive learning process that Chapter 11 is devoted to it.

≈≈≈

INTUITION IN ACTION
A STUDENT'S ANECDOTE

I have worked in the financial field for nearly two decades. I am an investment adviser specializing in new stock offerings. Each morning, my desk is covered with prospectuses of companies seeking a listing on one of the three major exchanges. Last year, I had taken a weekend course Laura offered on using intuition to improve decision making. I didn't tell my friends in the investment community that I was going to attend. Somehow intuition seemed out of place with the kind of sophisticated analysis and "number crunching" I am recognized for.

Still, I was greatly impressed by the discovery of my latent intuitive abilities in this course. So, despite the teasing of my secretary, I now began every morning with a ritual for which she has named me Karnac the Magnificent, after the old Johnny Carson routine. Before touching any of the company files, I jotted down notes on a legal pad and gave them to my secretary to type up. Only after I had finished making notes did I open the first file.

Now, on this particular Monday morning, I was about to begin making notes for the first file in the stack. In my mind's eye, I visualized a rabbit ready to start skiing down a mountain. The image seemed ludicrous, a little like Alice in Wonderland, but I jotted it down anyway. I'd learned from Laura not to dismiss my intuitive impressions, however outlandish they might seem at the time.

The rabbit started at the top of a very high mountain and quickly raced to the bottom. It remained there for what felt to me like weeks before beginning a slow climb to an even higher mountaintop. All of a sudden I became aware of the five fingers of my left hand. I wrote this all down, then started my day's work. I opened the company file and began sifting through the brochures. I noticed a home-and-garden supply company and thought, "Peter Rabbit." Doing some quick background research, I discovered most analysts thought this new issue was going to be a "hot stock."

Minutes before the exchange was to open for trading, I decided how many shares to buy. Apparently I was too late, because initial demand for the company's stock was so strong that the opening was delayed for over an hour. When the stock finally began trading on my computer screen, I kicked myself. It had skyrocketed over 25 percent from its initial offering price. The stock surged even more during the first hour of trading. There weren't enough shares to keep up with demand, and by noon the stock had doubled in price.

Having missed my first "opportunity," I decided to wait. I remembered my rabbit and recalled that the rabbit skied *down* the mountain. Sure enough, after several heady days the stock became volatile and began to plummet precipitously. Less than a week later, and fewer than three weeks since the first day, the stock had fallen below its original price. Week after week, the stock price continued to limp along, with frequent price slumps. While other analysts were now issuing twenty-twenty hindsight reports "explaining" the company's demise, I continued to follow the stock price closely.

A few weeks later, I punched up the closing prices of stocks on my monitor. I noticed that the home-and-garden company's stock had hit an all-time low: five dollars. I recalled the image of the five fingers of my left hand. I quickly reviewed my notes and verified my intuitive impressions. The next morning I placed a large buy order at the open. By the end of that day, the stock price had closed up strongly.

I continued to buy shares as the stock price kept climbing. After a few months, the stock surpassed its original price and advanced to new highs. Eventually I sold out for what people in the financial world call "a killing." My secretary no longer teases me.

≈≈≈

~~~~~~

- 5 -

WITHOUT FURTHER ADO

PLUMBING YOUR UNCONSCIOUS

We are about do some unconscious excavating of sorts. Don't "read into" the following exercise. It doesn't have a point. The purpose is simply to get you in a relaxed and receptive frame of mind.

~~~

EXERCISE 3
WARMING UP

Have your tape recorder or notebook handy. Take a moment to notice what you're sensing. Take a deep breath.

Allow your senses to become unfocused as you focus on your breathing. As you read these words, allow your senses to begin to wander. Follow one of your senses anywhere it wants to go.

Continue doing this for a few minutes. Record all your impressions, and later transcribe them in your intuition notebook under the heading Exercise 3.

~~~

Now that you're "centered," do the following exercise conscientiously. I'm keeping you in the dark on purpose. Just do the exercise.

≋

EXERCISE 4
INTUITIVE ASSOCIATIONS

Have your tape recorder or notebook handy. Take a moment to notice what you're sensing. Take another moment to do anything that helps you *dissociate* from those senses.

Do whatever you feel will be most effective to create a moment in which you're not sure what you're sensing: take a deep breath, stretch, or even scream and jump around madly.

When you're ready, sit down to respond to the following "triggers." This is like one of those Rorschach inkblot tests—say the first relevant thing that comes to mind. For example, if the trigger calls for a color and the first thing that comes to mind is a taste, wait until you pick up a color.

Spend no more than a few seconds on each trigger. If no response comes to you, make one up.

Here they are:

- a man's name
- a woman's name
- the name of an animal
- the name of a river
- a location
- a length of time
- a food
- a color
- a weapon
- a cure or remedy
- a wish
- a fear
- a memory

If you feel yourself "holding back" or trying to think about the choices, go through the list more than once. Record all your responses. Transcribe them in your intuition notebook under the heading Exercise 4. We will refer to these impressions again in another exercise.

≋

WHAT DOES ALL THIS MEAN?

I'll explain what you've done in this exercise in a few chapters. *Don't peek ahead.* For now, be patient. If you would like to compare your responses with those of one of my students, here's a student's trial:

- a man's name: Zach
- a woman's name: Jane
- the name of an animal: Rose, a donkey
- the name of a river: the Danube
- a location: Boston
- a length of time: one year
- a food: fragrant herbs
- a color: yellow
- a weapon: open hands
- a cure or remedy: strength; spinach
- a wish: a diamond
- a fear: failure
- a memory: rocking back and forth in a hammock and singing, "Swing low, sweet chariot, coming for to carry me home . . ."

HOW DID YOU FEEL?

Consciously you may have been annoyed that you were being asked to do a seemingly "pointless" exercise. Your unconscious, however, understood precisely what was being asked of it.

I will tell you now that I selected these thirteen triggers simply because they are evocative. Again, we will be returning to this exercise shortly. Before we do so, however, we need to discuss what it means to ask a question.

INTUITION IN ACTION
A TRUE STORY

When I was in my twenties, I was invited to speak to a group of business-people, scientists, and fellow intuitives on the subject of intuition. We shared some amazing stories of very practical, down-to-earth uses of intu-ition. Here is my favorite.

Many years ago a group of intuitives being researched at Stanford were asked to predict the price of silver for a businessman. They were not told who this mysterious person was.

To provide some "scientific" checkpoints, a simple computer program was set up that generated random images assigned the values up, down, and stays the same. Instead of predicting a price—which might have interfered with pure intuition—they predicted what image the computer would associate with a certain price movement. Each day the computer would change the random images, and each day the intuitives would select one that represented the price of silver.

For an astonishingly long time, the group correctly predicted the movement of the silver market. In baseball terms, they were batting prac-tically a thousand!

Eventually, his curiosity got the better of him and the anonymous employer wanted to meet the intuitives who were predicting a market they knew nothing about. Equally curious, the intuitives agreed.

It was dislike at first sight. The next day, the intuitives went back to work. And, for the first time, each one predicted silver prices *incorrectly*. They continued to "mess up" for weeks. The statisticians on hand announced that for all practical purposes what they were observing was mathematically impossible. In the next few weeks the group of intuitives batted a "perfect" zero!

After meeting the man and tracking a dislike to him, their subcon-scious minds decided to stop providing him with the right answers. But before this happened, they had helped him corner the silver market. He wound up losing millions of dollars.

- 6 -

THE ART OF
ASKING QUESTIONS

BE CAREFUL WHAT YOU WISH FOR—YOU MAY GET IT

To paraphrase this sage advice, you must be careful what questions you ask of your intuition, because you will surely answer them.

One of the frustrating things about working with computers is that they do only what you tell them to do. If a computer malfunctions, it's because your instructions were not correct. In a sense, your intuition is like that. It answers precisely the question before it. If you want to get the right answer, you'd better be sure you've asked the right question.

Since we'll be spending the rest of this book answering the three questions you asked in Chapter 4, we need to be absolutely sure you've worded them correctly.

AN ANCIENT ILLUSTRATION

Perhaps the most famous example of an ambiguous question put to an intuitive occurred in ancient Greece. A powerful ruler, about to invade the lands of an enemy kingdom, asked the Oracle at Delphi whether a great battle would be won. The Oracle responded in the affirmative.

The Oracle was correct; a great battle *was* won. Unfortunately for the king, it was won by his rival. Had he known as much as you now do about asking questions, he would have asked a question along the lines of this: "Will I *successfully* invade my rival's kingdom tomorrow?" Or better yet: "Will I successfully invade my rival's kingdom tomorrow *at an acceptable cost?*"

BACK TO THE PRESENT

As it was for the unfortunate monarch, it's easy for us to ask questions we don't intend to ask.

Let's take a simple example. Suppose you were in a whimsical mood, and the first question you asked was Will it rain tomorrow? The answer must be yes: *of course* it will rain tomorrow—somewhere!

INTUITION IN ACTION
AN ANECDOTE

I was in the front passenger seat of a car. My friend was driving us from Rome to Florence for a trade show. In Italy I often took on the habits of the Italians in not wearing my seat belt, so as the rain started methodically beating down on the roof of the car, I fell asleep without my seat belt on. I woke up to the screaming voice of my mother: "Put your seat belt on now!" Half asleep, I nonetheless immediately reached to fasten my seat belt. A second later I was knocked unconscious by the impact of the crash. The truck in front of us had stopped suddenly, and with the wet roads the driver of our car had been unable to brake effectively.

The driver of the truck disentangled me from the car and lifted me out. Shock was setting in as I asked if there had been any casualties and promptly forgot the answer to my question.

The next thing I remember is being on the table in the emergency room of the town hospital with Italian voices traveling in the air above me, very confused but with a pocket of clarity when I told them that my blood pressure was normally low and that I did not think I was bleeding internally so please to wait before operating. Thank goodness, they did.

No one was severely hurt: The driver, saved by the steering wheel, suffered only a concussion and cracked ribs, while I had sprained limbs. But without the seat belt it would have been an entirely different story.

People actually came to look at the car in the small town where the accident had happened, and a few stopped by the hospital to admire the unlikely survivors. I thought they were funny until I was discharged and went to see the car. The front was smashed like an accordion, and the top and back were buckled from the impact. I was struck by the miracle of my survival and the warning from my mother, who had died twelve years before.

A QUESTION PROPERLY PHRASED IS HALF ANSWERED

I am paraphrasing the old saying that a problem properly defined is half solved. The same is true of your questions. Understanding what you're asking often reveals much of the answer.

Now, a *bad* question is one different from the one you intended to ask. Often such questions are ambiguous and can be interpreted in more than one way.

Let's examine some misleading simple questions to see the unintended ambiguity lurking beneath them.

EXERCISE 5
REFINING AMBIGUOUS QUESTIONS

The following questions are all ambiguous in one way or another. Spend a few minutes considering the sources of their ambiguity and then formulate one or two more precise variations for each.
Here are the questions:

- Will I have enough money?
- Will I be happy?
- Should I take the new job?
- Should I become an artist?
- Will I get married and have children?

Jot down your thoughts in your intuition notebook. Please do this before reading the following discussion. Remember to label your notes Exercise 5.

EXPLORING THIS EXERCISE

What follows is a brief, and by no means complete, exploration of each question. You will undoubtedly think of additional points.

- *Will I have enough money?*

  Enough is a sly word. How much is enough? Enough to pay your basic bills? Enough to impress your neighbors? By what measure will you know you finally have enough?

  More specific variations might be something like the following: "When (or how) will I be financially secure enough to retire?" or "When will I be able to comfortably afford the kind of lifestyle I want?"

  Even these questions can have surprising twists. For example, perhaps you will have enough money in ten years to retire, but you will have become so interested in your work that you will not want to take time off, much less retire. Thank heaven the question wasn't phrased "When will I stop working?" or "When will I retire?" if what you really want to ask is "When will I be financially able to retire?"

- *Will I be happy?*

  You could get a head injury—knock on wood—that limits your ability to worry and thereby become "happy." Or you might become morally corrupt—knock on wood—not care about anything, and thereby become "happy."

  As you can see, happiness even as an end state is not without its complications. You might try to refine your question, as in "When will all the elements in my life come together in a satisfying way?" or "How do I create happiness in my life?" or "What impedes my being happy?"

  If the response indicates that you will never be happy, these questions still leave room for an answer like "I don't see your being able to be satisfied because doing so would require letting down your guard. Since you already feel exposed, you would need to work on that to become happy."

- *Should I take the new job?*

  The word *should* poses problems. Whether you should or not depends on your basis of evaluation. Consider the following variations of this question:

· "Should I take the new job if job security is my primary goal?"
· "Should I take the new job if experience rather than compensation is my primary criterion?"
· "Should I take the new job if I want to spend more time with my family?"

Your answer will probably reflect many such conscious—or unconscious—subquestions. As you can see, you must first think through *why* you want to change jobs and what you think the new job will do for you. Only then will you be in a position to ask whether your positive expectations will be fulfilled.

· *Should I become an artist?*
Other questions that pose difficulties are those that involve choices. In this question, for example, you could love being an artist without being particularly successful. If you want success as a criterion, you must incorporate it into the question: "Will I be successful as an artist?"
Even then, what do you mean by *success*? How is it measured? Perhaps a better question would be the following: "What issues do I need to evaluate in deciding whether or not to become an artist?"

· *Will I get married and have children?*
Compound questions present problems, since the answer to one half could be yes and the other no. A better question would be "What kind of family will I create and with whom?"

As you can see, formulating your question is not simply a matter of grammatical or semantic or philosophical correctness. In preparing and phrasing a question just so, you invest a great deal of feeling and emotion as well as logic.

≈

EXERCISE 6
BECOMING BETTER ACQUAINTED WITH YOURSELF

Take a long, deep breath. Allow your mind to relax back to the places in yourself where you hold memory. Trust that your unconscious will generate memories that provide the information you need to answer the question you've asked.

Allow yourself to get all the components of what is meaningful about the question listed for this exercise on page 38—but don't look until you've completed this exercise!

As you read this, allow yourself to stop every time your perceptions hit a memory. Record the memory or feeling. When your perceptions want to travel, allow them to until you hit another memory.

Don't worry about whether it's a "real" memory or you're just making it up.

Write down at least four memories in your intuition notebook.

When you feel complete with the exercise, turn to page 38 to see what question you were describing.

≈≈≈

ONE STUDENT'S RESPONSE

The following was produced by a male in his early fifties:

I remember my mother's explaining something to me when I was a child. I loved the feeling of her attention reaching inside of me to help me understand. I didn't really care about what she was explaining. I cared about the bubble of time with just the two of us inside it.

Sitting at a table with lots of people. I want to get away. I can't even ignore them because they ask me to respond to things. Dinner is served, and it's disappointing.

I am standing on the beach in Martha's Vineyard. The waves are carrying me out. The conversation of my friends behind me is holding me in place. There is both a melancholy and a sense of expectation and excitement. I feel changed.

≈≈≈

INTUITION IN ACTION
A STUDENT'S ANECDOTE

I took one of Laura's weekend workshops, and, even though she had instructed us to limit our activities during the workshop, I couldn't resist going to a dinner party I had been invited to. As I filled a plate with food at the buffet, I suddenly noticed that I was feeling somewhat "spacey." I couldn't catch hold of my thoughts or my awareness of the things around me. I had a few conversations and ate a little and then went home.

The host called me the next day to tell me that a gentleman I had spoken with at the party was intrigued by me. Apparently I had congratulated him (I couldn't honestly recall having done this) on opening his own firm. What puzzled him was that he had just decided to go into business for himself that morning. He had wanted to keep his plans a secret from his current employer for the moment, so he hadn't revealed them to anyone other than his wife and his prospective partner. He couldn't figure out how I knew about his plans if nobody had spoken to me about them.

When I told him about Laura's intuitive training, he asked for her number. He wound up taking one of her workshops the next summer. He now incorporates many intuitive techniques in his decision-making process and attributes much of the success of his thriving firm to them.

≈≈≈

THE SAMPLE STUDENT'S EVALUATION

Keep in mind that this man's questions were different from yours. Here is how he revised his question to make it more meaningful:

Of course I had to ask a broad question just to go against orders, and wouldn't you know that that would be the question I would have to look at first. The question was "What is the meaning of my struggle?" I didn't want to make it any more specific, just in case someone else would look at my question.

The first memory is about a hunger for intimacy that I had as a child, and how that hunger was filled. The second memory is about life outside that bubble being "disappointing." The third response is about the tension between reality and possibility, the past and the future. A reminder that longing can be for the past or

Response to **Exercise 6:** The question you responded to with your memories was simply this: "What is the essence of the questions I'm asking?"

for the future and that satisfaction can only be found in the present. I remind myself that I can change in the present.

I think I will change my question to read "How can I change right now to experience the most satisfaction in my life?"

THE THREE REQUIREMENTS OF GOOD QUESTIONS

A *good* question, then, is one you intended to ask. As in when you are working with a computer, you must direct your intuitive awareness carefully. Good questions—again, those for which we can generate useful information—satisfy three requirements.

First, each question must be specific and unambiguous so that a precise answer is possible. To clarify our previous example about whether it would rain, we would need to add a qualifying phrase: "Will it rain tomorrow *in Chicago*?"

Second, each question should be simple rather than compound. Let's say a woman is pregnant, unbeknownst to her. If her question is "Will I get pregnant soon and have a baby?" her intuition may respond with a negative, since she is *already* pregnant. Your intuition is confused by this compound question since the first half is false while the second half is true. (Incidentally, if your intuition is faced with a compound question, it will typically address the first half.)

Third, each question should be directly relevant to the issue you want to know about. In other words, know what you're asking.

Let's say a woman asks the question "Will I meet the man of my dreams?" If the man of her dreams is someone she knows, she may get a negative intuitive response. She will not meet the man of her dreams because she has *already* met him! It would be better to start off with the initial question "Do I already know the man of my dreams?" Or she could ask, "When will I meet the man of my dreams?"

To take a business example, don't ask the question "Is Cyber-Tech Corporation a good company?" when what you actually want to know is whether CyberTech Corporation stock is a good *investment.* Even more precisely, you probably want to know whether it will be a good investment *over a given time horizon.* A stock that might make an excellent short-term investment could prove to be a dud in the long run.

≈

EXERCISE 7
REVISING YOUR THREE QUESTIONS

In light of our discussion, review each of your three questions from Exercise 2 to make sure it satisfies the requirements just listed: specific, simple, and directly relevant.

Read each edited question out loud. While your intuition does not need spoken questions, hearing them once will remind you of their precise wording.

As we advised in Chapter 4, don't forget to ask a variety of questions, and ones whose outcome you will know in the next year or two at the longest. The feedback you get from answering them successfully—as I know you will!—will give you greater confidence in your growing intuitive ability.

If you'd like further ideas on useful questions to ask, feel free to glance ahead to "Other Useful Questions" in Chapter 25.

Rewrite your list and label this Exercise 7 in your intuition notebook.

Keep up the good work. Before you know it, you will be giving your first reading!

≈

AN IMPORTANT REMINDER

We will be spending the rest of the book answering the three questions you've listed in this exercise. Reread this chapter and the previous one closely and make sure you've carried out my instructions to the letter.

I hate to be a nudge, but it would be a shame if you spent a great deal of time in the next few weeks working through exercises only to discover that you were answering questions you didn't intend to ask.

INTUITION IN ACTION
A STUDENT'S ANECDOTE

Since learning to better use my intuition, I am very aware of my life's running in cycles. Sometimes I focus my intuition on love, while at other times my focus might be money, or my career, or my friends.

Nine years ago, when I started training my intuition, all my worries centered on love. As a result, my intuitive focus was on information about potential relationships. At first I got "hits" about what I needed to look at personally that was getting in the way of my finding love.

At one point a memory started to run in my head over and over. At first it made no sense. Then it connected with another memory, and then the memories got stuck on a name. I became very fond of the name Kirk because it was running through my head so much.

On a lark I called an old friend from high school. It wasn't until I had seen her a few times that I met her husband's brother, Kirk. I hated him on first sight. Yet now we have been happily married for five years.

My husband has not trained his intuition and was initially a skeptic. During our bumpy first year of marriage, I correctly intuited many things about Kirk, from what he had had for lunch to the fact that he had pneumonia. I learned, however, that he felt my sharing personal intuitions with him was sometimes intrusive. Now I confine my intuitive remarks to answering his questions. As a trial attorney, he always asks me questions before trial, such as "Are there any surprises in court today?"

Intuition has given me a greater feeling of control over my life and choices. Now when my broker tells me to buy a stock, I write the name down and look for myself; then I ask him more about the company. Only then do I make my decision. I feel I can be informed about subjects that I was dependent on other people to inform me about before.

- 7 -

CONGRATULATIONS ON
YOUR FIRST READING

A SECRET REVEALED: YOU'VE *ALREADY* GIVEN
YOUR FIRST READING

You may recall that in Chapter 5, I asked you to respond to a series of "triggers" in Exercise 4. At the time, I intentionally kept you in the dark about the purpose of the exercise.

Well, here it is: You were giving a reading in response to a question. Of course, you weren't aware of that, were you? At least not *consciously*. To see what question you were answering, turn now to the response to Exercise 8 (which follows shortly) on page 44.

WAIT A SECOND!

At this point, you may be saying to yourself, "Hold on! Is Laura saying I just gave an intuitive reading?"

That is *exactly* what I'm saying.

Now, I don't want to give you the impression that the association exercise is the way you give a reading. It isn't. Moreover, it would be a fair objection to argue that your responses in this exercise don't, in themselves, constitute an answer to the question we posed.

True enough. You still need to translate your impressions individually and then see what they mean collectively. You'll learn how to do this later. Nonetheless, for now let me assure you that doing a reading is not significantly more complicated than what you've already done.

In fact, without further instruction it would be a good exercise at this point for you to make whatever sense you can from your responses. Just do the best you can, as we'll be returning to this skill many times in the coming chapters.

≈≈≈

EXERCISE 8
MAKING SENSE OF YOUR INTUITIVE IMPRESSIONS

Looking over your list of responses from Exercise 4, what do you notice regarding each term? Now that you know what the question is (again, see the key to this exercise on page 44), I would like you to *justify* each response as a meaningful answer. It may seem that for one or more responses you must stretch your interpretation to "fit" the question. That's fine.

As always, record your answers. Don't worry if you sound awkward, this is the first reading you've done.

After you've reviewed your intuitive responses individually, look at them as a group. What do the impressions have in common? What over-all themes emerge?

Don't look merely for obvious themes; some can be quite subtle. For example, you may get the sounds of the following words: *tire, total,* and *terrific.* These are all *t* sounds. That may or may not be a significant clue.

Again, tape-record yourself if at all possible. Speak continuously—doing so gives your conscious, reasoning mind less time to interfere with the unconscious flow.

If you are writing your responses, write continuously, making sure you are in a comfortable position to do so.

Look at the fragments you received during your reading in Exercise 4. Notice the meaning each impression has *for you.* From this information, try to piece together an answer to this question. Remember to use your intuition notebook.

≈≈≈

REVIEWING ONE STUDENT'S READING

In Chapter 5, I gave you a transcription of one student's responses to Exercise 4. What follows is a transcription of her reading as she made sense of her associations after having looked at the question given below for Exercise 8.

> Jane is my name, and Zach is my husband's name. I just spoke with good friends of ours in Boston who have two children. They asked me to be their youngest child's godmother. Herbs grow in bunches. Yellow is the sun, without which nothing could grow. Maybe I'll have a son. A child is more precious than a diamond. The Danube means love. One year is self-explanatory. "Swing low, sweet chariot, coming for to carry me home." The image of the hammock reminds me of a baby in the womb. I would say I will probably have a child in the next year.

Don't intellectualize your responses. Allow your impressions to bring up other meaningful or suggestive associations.

WHY WE DID IT THAT WAY

The reason I didn't tell you in Exercise 4 that you were going to give a reading is that many students instantly throw up all kinds of blocks: "I don't know how to give a reading yet." "How can I answer a question I haven't seen?"

These conscious (as well as other unconscious) doubts interfere with the smooth functioning of your intuitive process. I needed you to be open to your intuitive impressions.

Notice that it was not necessary for your conscious mind to be aware of what you were doing intuitively. Once you gain more confidence in your intuitive powers, you will not need to bypass your conscious mind. Indeed, our goal is to give you

Response to **Exercise 8:** Here is the question your intuition gathered information for: "How will my life be different one year from now?" under Exercise 4.

conscious control over a process that is currently almost exclusively unconscious.

In the coming chapters I'll ask you to do other exercises whose point may not be immediately clear. Simply do them to the best of your ability—and trust that you're doing them correctly.

- 8 -

You Already Know Everything

The Forgotten Sense

Intuition is a capacity you're born with as a human being, like the capacity for language or thinking or appreciating music. Intuition is not a power one acquires. It's an integral part of every human mental, emotional, and psychical process.

Each moment—right now—you receive information intuitively; you're simply unaware of the process. You use your intuition in all those practical reasoned decisions you make every day, from choices as mundane as what to eat for dinner to what to major in or who to marry.

The trick to using your intuition more effectively is to bring the unconscious data it supplies to a place where your conscious mind can interpret it. It takes work and guidance to put this unconscious process under control. I'll show you how to do that. In a sense, this book is about developing awareness of an ability you already have and use.

Do You Remember the Old *Kung Fu* Television Series?

In the opening flashback episode of the TV series *Kung Fu,* the young David Carradine character has just been admitted into a secret Chinese temple where kung fu is taught. As he sweeps the dirt floor in the courtyard, he encounters one of the masters. The boy is surprised to discover that the man is blind, for he seems to get around as well as everyone else.

The sage tells him that blindness is not such a handicap, especially since it has allowed him to develop his other senses. To illustrate his point, he asks the boy whether he is aware of the tiny grasshopper silently sitting near his bare feet.

The boy looks down at his feet just as the grasshopper jumps away. He looks up to the master and asks, "Old Man, how is it you can hear the grasshopper at your feet?" The sage responds, "Young man, how is it you cannot?"

When people ask me how I became so intuitive, I am sometimes tempted to ask the same question: "How is it you are not?" Of course, like the sage, I am being somewhat facetious, since I am aware it's not always easy or even natural for us to do "natural" things.

I have yet to meet a person who is not intuitive. Are some people more so than others? Certainly. Some individuals are naturally more gifted in intuitive reasoning while others are more gifted as logicians, painters, or writers.

IF YOU'RE ALREADY INTUITIVE, WHY DO YOU NEED THIS BOOK?

You may be wondering why, if intuition is an innate ability that you use all the time, is this book necessary? Why, you might ask, should we make work for ourselves if we are already naturally intuitive? A good question (and, take my word, I'm one who most strongly believes in taking the path of least resistance).

In the first place, until now, using your intuition may have been a hit-or-miss proposition. The skill comes in knowing how to access and apply it *effectively*. Learning to understand the information you receive intuitively requires structure, just as thinking is improved with the structure that logic provides. Whatever native intuitive skills you've retained from your childhood, you can develop them, like any other skill, with guidance and practice. You'll learn how to tap this unlimited information-gathering faculty at will.

Moreover, intuition is a more powerful tool if it's not lost among all the other components of our decision making. The same is true of the emotions and the intellect. If we know what we are reacting to and why, we can make clearer rational decisions. It always amazes me that intuition and irrationality or "emotionality" are linked, since most of our decisions are an amalgam of diverse, and often conflicting, facts, feelings, thoughts, and memories.

Finally, becoming aware of your intuitive "hits" in a conscious way allows you to let intuition data supplement the other data you use to make decisions. Training intuition also trains the pure use of logic and emotion because training intuition helps you identify each process as separate, thereby enabling you to use the different capacities together more effectively.

INTUITION IN ACTION
AN ANECDOTE

Many years ago, my husband and I were looking for an apartment in New York City. My father had naturally assumed that I would live near him on Park Avenue. Looking through the Sunday *New York Times* real estate section, I spotted an ad I liked. Although the apartment was in a neighborhood I had never been to in all my years as a New Yorker, something drew me to it, so I went down to see it. The neighborhood was desolate by New York standards, but I still put a very low bid on two adjacent apartments.

To my utter amazement, the bid was accepted. I bought the two apartments in what several years later became one of the hottest neighborhoods in New York.

I later found out that my price was accepted because the building needed to sell two more apartments to qualify for their certificate of occupancy, and I had bid on the needed two.

IS THE MONSTER REAL?

We are all open to receiving intuitive information during childhood. Because we live in a society that teaches us to distrust anything but visible, tangible, "scientific" logic, however, this ability is trained out of us as we "grow up." This ability was never trained out of me.

As children we treat all our perceptions as real. Because our intuition is raw and untrained, we use it unconsciously to pick up only data that confirm our fears or wishes. We accept these perceptions unquestioningly because we are not aware they were picked up by our intuition. When a shadow on a bedroom wall at night appears to be a monster, children don't ask, "Is the monster real?" They ask, "Will it hurt me?"

Nor is the monster a vague creation. It has texture and purpose and is often a detailed and accurate representation of the stresses or threats in the child's life. If you ask the child what will make the monster go away, you will often get a detailed and accurate metaphor for the cure. The child's unconscious knows.

Adults, of course, are more "realistic." So children who tell their parents that they "saw" a monster are teased for their "imaginary" fears. Little do the parents realize that the children's unconscious may very well have presented a complex, abstract fear (say, of an adult's hidden rage) in the tangible symbol of something children can relate to: a monster.

Once we reach adulthood, most of us just know we are afraid, without the details to describe the fear and give us a handle on the remedy. Sometimes we project the fear onto something "real," such as flying or relationships. Because we have lost touch with our ability to fantasize and pretend, we have ironically cut ourselves off from our unconscious ability to provide us with meaning when, with intellectual maturity, it is potentially most useful to us.

At a very young age, then, we learn to distrust our intuition. As we grow up, we learn to judge data as real or pertinent or objective, and to weed out what is not real by society's standards. Over the years, this mental censoring becomes an unconscious, automatic process. Because most people have repressed their intuitive faculty since childhood, all intuition training must begin with noticing which of your perceptions you imagine and which ones you ignore.

LEARN TO RECOGNIZE YOUR INTUITION

Another reason you don't recognize intuition is that it speaks a different language. Intuition is often symbolic and fragmentary. Only on rare occasions does it speak in complete sentences. What's more, intuitive information often "does not make sense," especially when it involves the future. As a result, we train ourselves to dismiss it.

One morning, an actress friend of mine avoided her usual cappuccino on the set of her movie. She "felt strange" about drinking it so she didn't, even though she relies on two liberal cups of a beverage with caffeine to jump-start her day. Later that afternoon the whole set came down with a case of dysentery from the milk in the cappuccino, which was apparently tainted. The actress had saved herself a bout of illness by following her intuition even though there was no objective "reason" to avoid her daily cappuccino.

WE ARE NEVER PURELY EMOTIONAL OR PURELY LOGICAL OR PURELY INTUITIVE

Yet another problem is that, by the time you reach adulthood, your intuition is so deeply interwoven in your other mental processes that you can no longer use it independently of your thoughts, feelings, knowledge, and seemingly logical decision-making processes. Just as logic can be clouded by feelings, intuition can be clouded by knowledge and logic.

Whether you realize it or not, your intuition plays a role in every decision you make. People not trained in the use of their intuition are usually most intuitive about the things in which they are engaged daily: their careers or areas of expertise. Doctors instinctively use their intuition in making diagnoses, just as businesspeople use theirs in assessing the merits of an investment.

People also tend to be intuitive in the areas of their emotional preoccupations. A person fearful about losing his job during a period of corporate layoffs, for example, is going to have intuitive antennae fully extended to pick up any sign of danger. The intuition of a new mother is going to be finely tuned to pick up any information about her child.

Your intuition is continually at work, even on such mundane matters as cooking meals. Let's say you're planning a dinner for later in the evening. You are trying to balance the tastes of your family and basic nutritional requirements within your time realities when suddenly, for no particular reason, you see a yam in your mind's eye. Although you've never been a big fan of yams, you decide to add them to your shopping list. At dinnertime your sister is delighted. "How did you know?" she asks, telling you she's hankered for some yams all week.

CULTIVATING AWARENESS

If you're among the living, you breathe all the time without thinking about it. In fact, as you flip the pages of this book, your body is executing unbelievably complex physical actions simply, efficiently, and unconsciously. Breathing is a part of what we do. It takes place, thankfully, in the background, so we can consciously attend to other matters.

Yet, as accomplished practitioners of yoga can attest, there are many advantages to reclaiming conscious control over our breathing functions. By doing one of the many practices that focus on breath, we can control pain, increase concentration, help the body relax, and even accelerate the healing process.

Similarly, as you read the pages of this book, you're utilizing a number of complex mental functions *without your conscious awareness.* Let's examine one such function: your memory. When your eyes encounter a word on the page, it is instantly compared with the tens of thousands of words stored in your memory bank. Along with that word, images and associations stored with it are retrieved by your memory and served up to your conscious mind.

Your intuition functions in much the same way. It serves up data to your conscious mind continuously, even though you're usually completely unaware of the process.

So the key to developing your intuition is no mystery. It's simply a matter of learning how and where to shift your attention.

- 9 -

ATTENTION SHIFT:
UNLOCKING YOUR INTUITION

QUICKLY—RIGHT NOW: WHAT ARE YOU SENSING?

As creatures increasingly cut off from our environment by high technology, we have lost touch with our senses as well as our intuition. Because we are continuously bombarded by stimuli, we have learned to edit out most of the information we receive. We also cannot escape the influence of our society, which defines, through our language and conventions, what is accepted as "real."

So let's begin to get reacquainted with our senses. As you read this book, what impressions are you receiving through your sense of touch? Perhaps you're aware of the weight of the book in your hands. Perhaps you're aware of your weight as you sit.

What impressions are you receiving through your sense of sight? Your sense of smell? Your sense of hearing?

Let's not forget your other internal sensations, such as your thoughts and feelings, moods and memories. All these sensations are sweeping over you, yet in any moment you are only consciously aware of a tiny part of them.

Your aim, as you learn to exercise your intuition and develop it into a practical tool, is not to become aware of *everything*. Rather, your goal is to become acutely, exquisitely alive to whatever you're sensing so that you can consciously allow it to fade into the background. Once this everyday "noise" recedes, you can employ your senses to gather intuitive information.

Simply Reporting Your Sensations May Be More Difficult Than It Sounds

Since your eventual goal is to gather and note intuitive information, you need to report your sensations *as you experience them.* This means you must develop the ability to speak or write continuously at the same time you're receiving impressions. The following exercise will allow you to experience this.

Exercise 9
Becoming a Mirror

This simple exercise is nothing more than reporting everything you're sensing and feeling and thinking—out loud.

Again, if a tape recorder is not handy, enlist a friend to transcribe your words. If you're transcribing for yourself—use a form of shorthand so you can keep up with the flow of your impressions.

Since you want to become aware of your intuition in your everyday activities, be natural. You can do this exercise seated or lying down. When you're ready, take several deep breaths.

To begin, simply start reporting what you're sensing in the moment. If you hear a car beeping outside, say so. If your nose itches, say so (feel free to scratch it). If you're hungry, say so.

The trick is to report everything you notice—out loud. Don't forget to report any thoughts, feelings, or memories that you become aware of.

- If you remember a bill you forgot to pay, say so.
- If a commercial jingle keeps replaying itself maddeningly in your head, say so.
- If you feel you aren't "getting anything," say so.
- And if you think this exercise is silly, say so.

As you do this, you'll find yourself tempted to edit sensations that seem trivial or confusing. You'll especially try to ignore impressions that "don't make sense."

Resist these temptations. Make every effort to speak or write continuously. This will force you to report accurately, without the interference and censoring of your conscious mind.

Remember that you're not "supposed" to receive any particular impressions or images or sensations—for all you know, the interference that bothers you may be valuable data.

Stop after a few minutes, or whenever there seems to be a natural break in your impressions.

Finally, if you feel stuck, take a deep breath and focus on any one of your senses or thoughts. Allow it to lead you to another sense or thought, and so on. Remember to use your intuition notebook.

≈≈≈

START SPEAKING AS SOON AS POSSIBLE AND SPEAK CONTINUOUSLY

It's important to begin speaking as soon as possible after a question is asked. If you slow down or pause, your reasoning mind will kick in and interfere with the stream of intuitive images. Don't worry about using proper grammar, or even making sense. Keep speaking even if you "lose the thread" of your impressions. Trust that your intuition will quickly pick up the ball.

≈≈≈

INTUITION IN ACTION
A PERSONAL ANECDOTE

A client had come to see me about how best to work with her multiple sclerosis. The disease had been causing severe muscle cramps, confining her to a wheelchair much of the time.

While looking at her body, I kept getting an image of a western movie I had seen the night before. I was very focused on the cowboy spurs at the heels of the protagonist. I kept pushing the image out of my mind, convinced that it was interference getting in the way of my intuition.

Fortunately, I reported this "interference" to the client, who in turn relayed the image to her doctor (brave woman). The image spurred (pun intended) the doctor to examine her heels, where he discovered bone spurs. He corrected for these and alleviated the woman's need for a wheelchair.

≈≈≈

ONE STUDENT'S RESPONSE

To give you an idea of the kind of detail you should report, compare your transcript with that of one of my students, a middle-aged male. He chose to do the exercise with his eyes closed—you needn't—and used a tape recorder, so what follows is a verbatim transcription of a two-minute session. He spoke virtually nonstop except for brief pauses (indicated by ellipses), usually when he took a breath.

I'm aware of my breath, the sound of my exhalations, the movement of my chest . . . my left cheekbone itches . . . I need a shave . . . my back feels straight . . . the room feels chilly . . . I taste my last sip of coffee . . . I can hear the hum of my computer's cooling fan . . . I'm a little stiff, need to exercise . . . I wonder whether I'm doing this correctly . . . a car outside my window . . . I'm hungry . . . my nose itches . . . I wonder what causes all these funny patterns in my eyeballs . . . bright flashes of light, like a private kaleidoscope . . . I feel my weight in this seat . . . did I say I'm hungry? . . . I don't see the point of this . . . I feel my right elbow . . . is this long enough? . . . this reminds me of a doctor's examination . . . cold stethoscope . . . how come I can't hear my heartbeat? . . . I hear the clock ticking on the wall . . .

AN INVALUABLE EXERCISE

Reporting your impressions without editing is such a vital skill that you may want to practice this exercise for several days before proceeding. You don't need to set aside time; use spare moments throughout the day.

- 10 -

There Are No Coincidences

Why Do You Notice What You Notice?

In the previous chapter you began becoming more aware of your surroundings. The point was not to become aware of everything (which would be impossible) but simply to notice what you're noticing.

Now, we all notice completely different things. Why do you notice what you notice while I notice other things? Most people believe the answer to that question is random occurrences. In other words, what they notice in any particular moment is a comparatively random or chance event. Here's what one student had to say:

> Well, I just notice what I notice. Things come to my attention. Sometimes I may be more aware of my surroundings through one sense or another, but I don't think there's any pattern or anything to it. I notice what I notice. It doesn't mean anything.

I think you'll agree that this is what most people would say. And most people are completely mistaken on this point.

What if—just what if—you notice what you notice *for a reason*?

Are You Open-minded?

We now come to what, for most of my students, is the most incredible aspect of intuition. Brace yourself, because I am about to ask you to accept a premise that will alter your perceptions. It may even force you to revise your notions of experience and reality.

Everything you perceive—everything you sense, or remember, or feel, or dream, or intuit, in short, everything you notice—has meaning. Everything.

Let's let that sink in for a moment. If you aren't trembling right now, the full import of that statement has not yet dawned on you. So let's explore the implications we can spin out of this premise.

EVERYTHING IS A SIGN

If you notice that your nose itches, that fact has meaning. If you notice the color of your skin, that fact has meaning. If you notice that you're noticing your noticing as you read these words, that too has meaning.

Nothing is random. Everything you notice is significant. In other words, there are no coincidences.

The more you think about that, the more it boggles the mind. Everything can be interpreted. There is nothing in life that doesn't have a meaning. When I walk blindly through the world, I notice that the energy in front of me is patterned; all I must do is walk into it. There is also a great part of my experience of the world that I structure, either consciously or unconsciously. Consciously I structure a meeting with my father; I call him up and say, "Let's meet." Unconsciously I structure a fight with my best friend for some other reason.

Every moment—past, present, and future—has a meaning. Every sign, every act, every deed, every thing we notice can be traced to the past and is being noticed in the present through the filter we're using in the moment. And everything we notice has an application and a meaning in the future. Here is an exercise that will help you apply this principle productively in your everyday life.

≈≈≈

EXERCISE 10
WHAT DO YOU NOTICE?

PART I

In a moment I will ask you to take your eyes off this page and look around the room. Not yet, but when I do ask you to look up, I want you to take the first thing your eye settles on and describe it in detail. Pretend that what you see evokes images, feelings, or even a story—and report the impressions and information you receive.

There is no right way to do this. You will be allowing this information to be descriptive of the answer to the question on page 60.

OK. Look up now. Describe the first thing you notice, and allow it to be your response to the question for this exercise. Report your impressions in detail.

PART II

Look over your response. Are your impressions positive or negative? Did you get a sense of yes or no? Does what you perceive (smell, see, taste, feel, imagine) change for the more positive or the less positive? What other clues did your intuition provide?

Record all your impressions and transcribe them in your intuition notebook under Exercise 10.

≈≈≈

ONE STUDENT'S RESPONSE

Here is how one student read his sealed question:

I notice a tin letter box with a pig painted on it full of mail. The pig is eating grass and looks happy. The pig walks away from the box full of things to do. A wolf is watching the pig, but they are separated by a fence. The sound of the air conditioner is bothering me. The pig keeps eating calmly, knowing that the wolf is no match for the fence between them. The pig has no need to go into the wolf's territory, and the wolf eventually dies of hunger from watching the pig in vain from the other side of the fence.

Here is how he interpreted his reading when he opened his envelope to reveal the question: "Will I be forced to sell my company at an unacceptable price?"

The tin letter box full of mail could be my company and all of its recent difficulties. The wolf is the prospective buyer waiting for our difficulties to drive down the price. The pig's walking away and the insurmountable protection provided by the fence give me the sense that the difficulties will be resolved and that the "wolf" will not get us. After all, the wolf dies because it didn't get what it wanted. The answer here is a clear no.

Allow your images to speak to you. Translate any metaphors into useful information. Don't overthink the process. As with an allegory, allow your imagery and metaphor to tell the story.

WHY WE DON'T NOTICE MORE

Now, you may be wondering how your mind copes with all the meaning around you without getting confused or even becoming crazy. Unless you're taking psychoactive drugs or have a very unstable personality, your subconscious mind is not going to allow your conscious mind to be overwhelmed. Out of the welter of information around us, your subconscious tells you what you should notice. It knows what is important for you, and it selects and coalesces information into a meaningful pattern.

WE GET SIGNS ALL THE TIME, AND IN A MILLION WAYS

Things are hitting us over the head all the time. But in our culture we are trained not to see them. When we get a thought, we don't allow ourselves to take the next step to make it tangible. You almost have to give yourself "head-hitting" moments. You might say to yourself during meditation, "Between 10:30 and 11:00 this morning, I'm going to notice what hits me over the head." You can take it off your head, you can look at it, and you can say, "Gee, is this useful for me?"

The problem in meditation for me as a practical person is that it tends to stay above the earth. I want information I can use. By selecting what you notice, you create information. But if you just notice and don't create something tangible, the information remains somehow unconscious and therefore not useful.

As I write this, I'm looking at a book on my bookshelf. There is a reason I'm looking at that particular object. The name Diane pops out at me. Perhaps I will meet a Diane the day after tomorrow. Perhaps Diane will be the name of my son's teacher next year. If I allow the title of every book I see up there on my bookshelf to represent everyone I'm going to meet, ultimately it will. My unconscious will choose those names that correspond to people I will meet or with whom I'll interact in some way.

We do this instinctively with the signs we believe in. We can also choose to do it in other ways. You can say, "OK, every number I see will be a winning lottery number." I'm not good enough to do that yet, or I would be a millionaire, but I'm sure it can be done.

INTUITION EXTENDS THE RANGE OF YOUR AWARENESS

We have been discussing the significance of what you notice in the world around you. Now, when most people speak of awareness, they see it as something fixed. They think we can be aware of our immediate surroundings but that's about it.

That is a misconception. Intuition can extend your awareness to an unlimited extent. With intuition you can "project" your awareness to any place and any time. Babies are born with boundless awareness because they are undifferentiated from the world around them. As a result, the data they receive has no form. These bits of data aren't information, much less information that can have a practical use. Our goal is applying our intuition to gain *useful* information.

It Comes Down to What We Choose to Notice

I sense that in every choice we make—even whether to walk down Sixth Avenue or Fifth Avenue—we're making a decision about what we encounter. We also make decisions about what we notice. Some people notice the interesting or attractive people on the street, others notice the garbage. Most of the time these are unconscious choices. Where we can really use the conscious mind as a tool is in noticing the choices that we make. If we find ourselves seeing only the negative, we can notice that preoccupation and look for the good.

You Are an Active Participant in the Creation of Your Reality

In a sense, we are always creating. Although we cannot will the signs we are going to *get,* we can will what they're going to *mean* to us. I suppose, to go back to my earlier example, that I can will myself to notice the word *Diane* in everything I see. But then the object of the exercise is to see the word *Diane.* If I will something to be predicted, the object of the exercise is to instruct my unconscious to select what will be pertinent in the future.

Further Speculations

This is a practical rather than a theoretical book, but this chapter is important to help you trust your intuition. If you aren't ready to trust, you may want to think about the ideas here more extensively. In Chapter 30 we will explore in greater detail some of the profound implications intuition has for our understanding of ourselves and the world.

DON'T TAKE MY WORD FOR IT

Everything—everything—you notice around you has significance. In other words, there is a reason you notice what you do and don't notice everything else. The trick is knowing what question the information is answering.

It's extremely difficult for most people to accept that everything they notice is significant. If you have trouble with this concept, begin by *pretending* that everything is a sign and look for the meaning. Having said that, I realize many people have trouble pretending, so in the next chapter we're going to practice what used to be child's play for you.

REMEMBERING HOW TO PRETEND

INTUITION IS LITERALLY CHILD'S PLAY

An important step in developing your intuitive awareness is learning to accept your extrasensory impressions. Relying on intuition means operating without the safety net of logic, common sense, and sensory experience. It isn't easy, but you can do it by pretending. If you pretend that everything has meaning, and look for an application of that meaning, you sift through what is meaningful and what is meaningless to identify signs for you.

But the first step is to pretend that my looking at this Perrier bottle on my desk next to my computer has meaning. Then, I either find the meaning or, as an intuitive, *allow* the meaning to come to me. I don't worry if it doesn't make immediate sense— symbols often don't.

The problem is that we use the same criteria to interpret symbols and intuitive information that we do to see if a virus responds to a drug in a laboratory. And you can't do that. Intuitive information cannot be repeated in some controlled experiment, any more than dreams repeat themselves with identical detail night after night. But that doesn't mean dreams don't provide information, and information that consistently repeats the same meaning or message. You can have a dream that doesn't make sense to you when you dream it. When you go back later, however, and reexamine it, the sense can become apparent.

Once again, the most important thing is to document what's significant to you in your environment by making a choice. For instance, you can say to yourself, "My symbols this week are going to be any flowers I see." Later your intuition notebook entries might read, "On Seventh Avenue I saw a pink flower, and then on Sixth Avenue I saw a yellow flower."

The same object noticed by two people can mean two very different things. Cats, for instance, do not mean the same thing to everybody. To a person who loves cats, they can be a sign of friendship or physical affection. To someone who doesn't, they might be a sign of bad luck.

You have to allow the meanings of your symbols to come to you, and this may take time. It also takes an open mind, even if at first you have to pretend that the symbols are significant. Allow things to be meaningful and they *become* meaningful.

≈≈≈

EXERCISE 11
THE SHIRT ON YOUR BACK

Pretend that the color of the shirt or blouse you're wearing is the answer to the question listed for this exercise.

Describe the color, any memories associated with it, what the color means for you in this moment, and how your perception of the color has changed during this exercise. Remember to use your intuition notebook. Turn now to page 66 and read the question. Justify your answer.

≈≈≈

ONE STUDENT'S RESPONSE

The following was done by a young woman in her early thirties:

Somewhere between aqua green and clear-day sky blue. I remember lying on the grass in my grandmother's garden as a child, looking up at this color and seeing the sky move above me while dreaming that I could really have all of my wishes. They would come walking out from behind the rosebush I could see out of the corner of my eye as I looked up. Blue was the color I saw outside my window over the large orange building that blocked my view of the city. I remember how the clear blue used to contrast with the brown-orange of my room. There was a safety in the brown-orange, but I also felt trapped by it and longed for the freedom of the blue.

In this moment I notice the green tint. It reminds me of sea glass. I used to love to find sea glass at the shore. The history that had rubbed what was once a chip of a beer bottle smooth and precious seemed magical to me.

In this moment the color of my blouse looks calm but pleasant. I notice the strength in the color more than I did when I began the exercise.

These intuitive impressions convey a strong sense of hopeful nostalgia. I would say that developing her intuition will very probably help this woman get in touch with a lost part of her childhood.

$$\approx$$

INTUITION IN ACTION
A STUDENT'S ANECDOTE

I was working on a baby who was born after only seven months in the womb. The baby was so tiny the nurses measured its weight in grams: 1200 (just over two and a half pounds). After two days, the baby needed not less oxygen, as we would have expected, but more. His need for oxygen increased steadily, and there was a great deal of discussion among the hospital staff about the cause of this alarming condition.

I had a feeling, a physical feeling, that the baby needed a larger breathing tube. After the situation continued to worsen, I told the neonatologist what I felt, and he said that it was unlikely and the risk of more bleeding into the baby's lungs far outweighed the slim chance that I was

Response to **Exercise 11:** The question you were responding to was this: "How will I change from doing this book?"

correct. I continued to get the feeling and continued to insist, and on the fifth day, when the baby looked as if he would die anyway, they changed the breathing tube and the baby immediately improved.

Another time there a baby who was born prematurely but who, at four pounds, was good sized (our unit sees babies that weigh less than a pound). He had lung disease, and he needed oxygen. He continued to need the oxygen, and we became worried because this was not appropriate for a baby of his size and maturity.

One day I was assigned to take care of this baby. That night I had a dream that the baby had a broken heart. In the dream I told him, "Silly, your lungs are sick, not your heart," but after I woke up, the dream stayed in my mind.

At work that day I was assigned to another baby. The dream prompted me to realize that the baby from the day before had no regular nurse to become bonded to. I talked to some of the other nurses, and we decided that the same nurses would always work with that baby so he would feel loved. After that, the baby recovered quickly, and the nurses caring for him really fell in love with him.

When the baby was going home, the father apologized to us for not bringing us all gifts, but the family couldn't afford to. He explained that while his wife was pregnant with the baby, he had had a massive heart attack. He was just thirty-four and had recently lost his job as a truck driver. They already had one child and were considering aborting this one, but they decided to rough out the financial difficulties and have the baby anyway.

I got goose bumps as he was telling me the story, and it clicked with the dream of the baby with the broken heart.

≋

WHY CHILDREN PRETEND

As children we had no trouble pretending. When we are children we know very little about the world around us, and we use pretend play as a way to experiment with knowing. We have no trouble making things up. We delight in playing make-believe.

My three-year-old is sure that the way to be a man is to have a sword and kill bad guys and to cook in his pretend kitchen wonderful treats for his collection of snakes. He is going to marry Fay Wray (who conquered King Kong), Thumbelina, a girl we met named Barry (whose back sports an enormous dragon tattoo), and, of course, me. All these things are very concrete for him, but they will change as he grows up and is exposed to more information.

As we become older and "mature," many of us lose touch with this important ability to pretend because of the overwhelming social pressures to be logical and sensible. Even young children are encouraged not to make things up. What's more, our ability to pretend and to create has been replaced to a large degree by technology, like videos and television and advertising, which gives our brains most of what they need to keep entertained.

All of this is too bad, because pretending performs some very useful functions. When we engage in a sport or play a game, for example, we are pretending it's important to get the football over the goal line or to checkmate our opponent's king. Pretending is also a valuable ability when learning a new skill. Before we master something, it helps to pretend that we've already acquired the skill. When learning a foreign language, for example, it helps to pretend that you're a native speaker.

Even modern science is based on pretending. Physicists and chemists pretend that matter is made of atoms. Mathematicians pretend that the sum of the interior angles of a triangle is 180 degrees. The amazing thing is that, starting from what might be called make-believe, modern science is actually able to understand and even mold reality.

Finally, we should note that pretending often precedes faith. Indeed, pretending often generates faith, and, before we know it, we no longer need to pretend.

INTUITIVE INFORMATION OFTEN DOES NOT MAKE SENSE— SO WE MUST PRETEND IT DOES

As long as we insist on our experience of the world making sense, we will deprive ourselves of valuable intuitive data. Our society's insistence on being "realistic" cuts us off from a large part of reality. Pretending and being able to make things up are important skills to cultivate as you gain control over your intuition.

Exercise 12 will help you get back in touch with a part of you that you may not have experienced since childhood. As always, you'll need a pen, your intuition notebook, and your tape recorder.

TRUST YOURSELF

Your reading in this exercise will be a natural extension of Exercise 11. The instructions will follow shortly. I make these observations here so they will not get in the way of the flow of your reading once you begin.

Read the following points once or twice. And then forget them. Trust that your unconscious mind will retain what you need to know for this exercise. You don't need to memorize this list in any event; we will be covering these points numerous times throughout the book.

- **Giving a reading is not taking a test—so don't worry about whether your impressions are "right" or "wrong."** When they think of intuition, most people think of using it to grasp "the right answer" immediately. Remember that intuition is an information-gathering process with which you gain ammunition to get at some version or approximation of "the truth."
- **Trust your intuition.** Don't try to "figure out" the answer. Simply allow yourself to notice the images or symbols and other impressions a question brings out in your intuition.
- **The impressions you receive don't have to make sense to you.** The impressions you get don't have to make sense with one another; they may even seem to be contradictory. This is normal—especially if you're responding to a question you know little or nothing about. Keep in mind that when someone else asks you a question, you may not consciously know anything about the topic. Moreover, many things may come through to your consciousness in the asker's symbols and internal

language, so be careful simply to *record* your information, not *judge* it.

- **Intuition is a natural sense, so you don't have to try to receive impressions.** You couldn't stop being intuitive this moment any more than you could stop hearing the sounds around you. Simply *allow* yourself to report what you're picking up in response to a question.
- **The idea is to make mistakes!** If you're not willing to make mistakes, you won't get to the place where you can tap your intuition. As you do this more and more, you'll discover that your intuition does not make mistakes. But that isn't to say that you won't make mistakes in interpreting intuitive information.
- **In short, record everything—even impressions that seem like interference.**
- **If you feel you aren't getting an intuitive response, make something up!** I'm serious. You'll be amazed at how accurate your "guesses" can be.

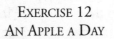

EXERCISE 12
AN APPLE A DAY

As you read these words, I want you to allow an apple to appear in the middle of the page before you. Don't "try." Indeed, there is nothing for you "to do." Simply allow the image to appear. If another image appears, *pretend* you see an apple. That's right, make one up!

Notice when you can first see the apple. Notice what it smells like. Notice how much heavier it makes the book you're holding. Notice its color. Allow yourself to perceive its size.

Now allow another apple to appear beside the first one. Again, if you can't see your apples, pretend that you can. Make them up.

Now, which apple is larger: your first or your second?

When you've decided this, turn to page 72 for the question you were reading. Remember to use your intuition notebook.

ONE STUDENT'S RESPONSE

As always, do not continue beyond this point until you've done the exercise. The following student response will reveal the question:

> I see a small, yellow apple with little black spots. The spots aren't imperfections; somehow they're endearing. I can't smell a fragrance, but the apple feels good in my hand. It's light but precious. In some moments it shrivels and then returns to its original beauty with a little effort of imagination.
>
> My second apple is red, large, bold. It has a fragrance that reminds me of apple blossoms. Its vibrancy excites me. I feel happy.

THE STUDENT'S INTERPRETATION

Here is how the student translated his reading:

> I don't think that this reading needs much interpretation. I was surprised to get a yellow apple and "light but precious"! I would say that the price of gold will rise tomorrow.

The student, incidentally, was correct.

For a dramatic illustration of the power of this technique for predicting financial markets, see the Intuition in Action story in Chapter 5. You might also recall the statement of billionaire investor George Soros I cited in Chapter 2.

HELPFUL HINTS

A reading often gives you the same answer in many ways. The student's second apple was bigger; it had fragrance, unlike the first apple; the feeling was happy. All these things indicated a clear yes to this student.

Many students ask, "Why do I need a metaphor? Why can't I just do a reading of the primary object or person directly?" The answer is that when people or issues are important to us, our emotions can get in the way. For example, there is less emotion attached to the question "Which apple is bigger, the first or the second?" than there is to the question "Will the price of gold go up or down tomorrow?" The apple is an innocuous surrogate on which we can more easily do a purely intuitive reading.

IF YOU'RE STILL SKEPTICAL

You might be asking yourself, If intuition is different from guessing, then why should this exercise work at all? The answer lies with your subconscious and its directive to take cues from the environment around you. You gave your subconscious a cue when you picked up this book. If you believe in intuition, you probably gave your subconscious the cues that you were going to allow yourself to function intuitively, and in doing so prepared to do a reading.

If you don't believe in intuition, you have two choices: Either you allow intuition to prove itself or you decide to prove that it doesn't work.

If you fall into the latter category, this exercise was probably not as fruitful as it was for those who fall in the former. Make a conscious choice to give intuition a chance.

I remember an intuition seminar I taught at Esalen Institute in California. A woman had chosen to take the workshop, convincing her husband to take it with her even though he didn't "believe in" intuition and wasn't interested in learning about it.

Response to **Exercise 12:** The question you were answering was this: Will the price of New York gold tomorrow close higher or lower than it did today?

- If your second apple was bigger than your first, you answered "higher."
- If your second apple was smaller than your first, you answered "lower."
- If your apples were the same size, you answered "no change."

To see whether your intuition was on target, check the price of New York (COMEX) gold in the financial section of tomorrow's paper.

You can do this exercise "blindfolded" with friends. Arbitrarily adopt signs that will indicate yes and no, and then let them ask you questions. This is a good exercise to get you in touch with your intuitive style.

It was no great surprise, then, that the first evening this man proved to be a very difficult student (it seems that every class needs at least one major skeptic to make things more interesting). We did an exercise in which we predicted the winners of a horse race, and he did poorly, proving to himself that intuition training has no merit. He discounted the many others who did well on the exercise with a lengthy discourse on the mathematics of probability and chance occurrences.

The next day we did an exercise in which you give a description of someone's life in great detail without knowing the person. This man was extremely resistant, so I pushed him into making the answers up. Perhaps to amuse himself, he did just that.

You can probably guess what happened next. He described the other person's life with such accuracy that he knew the make of his father's car and the school from which he had graduated.

He missed the next session of my class, and I asked his wife why he was absent. She told me that he had been frightened by the accuracy of the reading he had given. He now believed in intuition but didn't think it was right to get information in this manner.

I asked her to suggest to him that he was getting and using this information all the time; he simply was not conscious he was doing it. Wouldn't it be better, I told her to ask him rhetorically, to be aware of the information that he was acting on in making decisions so he could use it more productively?

Apparently this appealed to his sense of reason, and he returned to finish the course. I like to think that he not only trained his intuition but changed as a human being by becoming consciously aware of how deeply he was responding to his environment and the people in it.

As you do the exercises in this book, the message that you will allow yourself to use your intuition consciously will become clearer to your subconscious, and your readings will improve.

Even if you still doubt your intuitive powers, you probably generated some information in this exercise that was accurate. Look your information over and try to make it apply to the question. In doing so you may notice that you know more than you think you do.

EXERCISE 13
A QUICKIE

When you look up from this book, record your impressions in response to each of the following questions:

- What do you see?
- What do you hear?
- What do you taste?
- How do you feel?
- What do you smell?
- What is going through your mind?

Gather your impressions—they comprise your answer to the question at the bottom of page 76. As always, remember to use your intuition notebook.

ONE STUDENT'S RESPONSE

Here is the reading of one student for his question (again, he did not know which question he was reading at the time):

> The computer, noise outside. Work noise. I imagine from a restaurant. A little bit of bitterness surrounded by a good taste. I feel anxious in my chest but comfortable in my surroundings. I smell a good, cool smell, which is at the same time a little bit irritating. I am hoping that this is not my love question. I feel a little sad. I am thinking of my mother and the town she grew up in, where her parents still live and where I spent my childhood summers.

Here is how he interpreted this reading when he learned the question was "Will my girlfriend and I get married?"

> There are many conflicting images. Is the irritation worth the comfort? The "noise" of work is a reality for both of us. We are working so hard that we don't have time for each other. My

mother's parents have been married and in love for half a century. That is what I want, as well as the sense of family I had in my childhood.

If I had to give a yes/no answer now, I think that the answer would be no. I would like the answer to be yes, so I think that I have to work on spending more time with my girlfriend and address the irritation level, which has risen in the last few months. There is "a little bit of bitterness," but it is "surrounded by a good taste." The answer still may be no, but I want to give it a shot.

Remember always to look for possibilities and alternative scenarios in your readings. Life is rarely black and white.

BEWARE THE POWER OF MAKE-BELIEVE

It is perhaps easy for us as adults to dismiss statements that someone "just makes up." Yet one of my favorite illustrations of the power of make-believe is a wonderful short story by Jean-Paul Sartre. The narrator, a French Resistance fighter during World War II, describes in flashback a harrowing ordeal. He had been captured by the Germans and tortured for a week to reveal the location of his comrades. As stoic as he was patriotic, he endured unspeakable pain in silence.

Finally, however, he simply got *bored* with his torture. So, to amuse himself (like the husband at my seminar), and thinking he would thereby expedite his execution, the hero feigned a confession. "They're in the basement of the church," he lied, amusing himself by imagining the Germans storming a vacant church in a vain search for his compatriots.

He was astonished when, several hours later, his German captors returned not to execute him but to set him free! Apparently he had unwittingly revealed *precisely* where his fellow fighters had chosen to hide.

For Sartre, the moral of the story was undoubtedly something about cosmic humor and the existential plight of human beings. On a more profound level than the author was perhaps aware of, however, this story is a compelling dramatization of the truth we unknowingly utter when we "make things up."

- 12 -

RELYING ON INTUITION
CAN BE SCARY

CONSCIOUSLY USING INTUITION TAKES GUTS

It is sometimes glibly stated that you must "learn to trust" your
intuition. We often hear people advising others to "trust your
gut" or "trust your hunches." But using intuition takes a whole
lot more than trust, because sometimes you don't get feedback
until months or years later, when the person involved calls you up
and says, "Hey, you were right!"

Our intuitions must compete with our preconceptions about
how the world works, our bias in favor of "logic," and our overreliance on "common sense."

Here is a list of the more frequent ways people dismiss legiti-
mate intuitive insights:

- "That doesn't make sense."
- "That isn't logical."
- "I just made that up."
- "It simply isn't possible to know for sure what will happen
    in the future."
- "That can't be right."
- "This isn't realistic."
- "This is silly."

Response to **Exercise 13:** You were answering your Question 2.

How many of these expressions must you eliminate from your thinking?

≋

INTUITION IN ACTION
A STUDENT'S ANECDOTE

Before I was to be hospitalized for a hip replacement operation, I was having a meeting with the managerial staff of my company. For many years, we have used Laura's intuitive techniques as part of our strategy meetings.

We had all just put our questions on the table and were writing our impressions when I got the strong feeling that this would be my last meeting. I put my elbows on the table, rested my head on my hands, and stopped writing. A few other people, noticing my discomfort, stopped writing too. We shared our intuitions about my operation.

My partner told me he had an intuition that my heart was going to stop during surgery and that he was sure it was just his fear rather than his intuition speaking, so he hadn't mentioned it. I called Laura that evening. She told me that she saw the heart having more water than it should. I was going to cancel the operation when Laura suggested that I voice my concerns to my doctor (her usual advice for anything medical). He and I agreed that we would put a monitor directly into the heart, although it was a painful procedure, which had to be done while I was awake.

During the operation my heart began to have trouble, which was detected immediately by the monitor they had inserted. Apparently fluids had been administered too rapidly during surgery, and this had put pressure on my heart. The doctor later told me that if the monitor had not picked up the difficulty so quickly, my heart would probably have stopped completely and needed resuscitation to restart—a procedure that is not always successful. I probably would never have found out this much information had the doctor not been a family friend.

Although I have wonderful doctors whom I trust, I will never again leave my intuitions about myself unexplored. They are part of the information that I bring to any process.

≋

Learn to Suspend Judgment

I've been preparing you for some time now to accept the importance of being open to your intuitive impressions. You may feel uncomfortable or even silly about receiving and articulating intuitive impressions when your logical mind tells you that you can't possibly know anything about a topic on which you have no information.

You may hear an inner voice whisper, "This doesn't make sense." Don't ignore that voice—record it, and then move on. Accept *all* your impressions.

It's crucial that you become aware of how your logical mind tends to censor your intuitive impressions. A common way this happens is for your mind to label them as "interference," "projections," or "just my imagination." These labels are judgments. They are the result of your logical mind asserting itself when it's forced to work without information.

For this exercise, record all your impressions:

- If you can't get the letter *G* out of your head because it keeps intruding itself forcefully while you're awaiting "genuine" impressions, say so.
- If you can't hear yourself think because the car down the block keeps honking its horn, say so.
- If you feel a cramp in your left foot while speaking, say so. If you're "not getting anything" because you keep thinking about a pressing deadline at work, say so.

All these are valid impressions. Record everything you're thinking, feeling, sensing, or remembering when receiving impressions in response to a question—*everything!*

Exercise 14
Learning to Trust

At the bottom of page 80, there is a question listed for this exercise. Don't look at it until you've completed this exercise. Instead, I want you to pretend that you know the answer while you use all your senses to confirm it. As you read the rest of this exercise, pretend that your senses are already investigating the answer to the question asked on page 80.

You don't have to make any kind of conscious effort. You don't even have to think about it. Simply pretend that as you read my words your senses are perceiving the information you need to answer the question.

The idea is not to *guess* what the question or answer is. You want fragments of information that, when assembled, are meaningful to you and describe the qualities of the answer. These fragments don't have to make sense, nor do they have to follow any kind of logical pattern. After all, you don't even know what you're talking about.

Do you?

Now, as you pretend that you're able to perceive this question with all your senses, further pretend that everything you think, remember, smell, see, feel, taste, hear, or perceive in any other way is a fragment of information helpful in answering this question.

With either your pen or your recorder, begin to report all your impressions.

Take a deep breath and notice what you smell. Notice what you hear. Notice what you imagine.

Allow yourself to notice what emotion you're feeling in this moment, and what memories that emotion evokes.

Write all these impressions down.

Pretend that you're in a different place. Where are you? What are you doing? Who do you see around you? What's going on in the distant background?

Allow yourself to notice anything else in this moment. Let these senses have a life of their own, and let yourself notice them. You may taste something you're seeing or hear something you're smelling. Allow all your senses the freedom to interact and create, and notice what emotion you're feeling—right now.

Now, turn to page 80 to see the question for which you were gathering information. Remember to use your intuition notebook.

≋

DEVIL'S ADVOCATE

You know, I tried to record my interference as you suggested, but I was completely blocked and frustrated during this exercise! I just couldn't get in touch with my intuition.

No! You *assume* you were blocked. It may very well have been that the blocked feeling itself was your intuitive answer to the question! If you still get "interference," make it part of the process. Let's say you keep hearing a commercial jingle in your head while trying to get an intuitive reading on a particular question. Make the jingle part of your response to the question. If you must, pretend that the jingle is the answer.

Still, this is a common experience with students beginning their intuitive training. Since you may find it nearly impossible to resist the habit of labeling (i.e., dismissing) intuitive impressions—don't! In other words, **deliberately label your impressions as you articulate them.** Divide them into three categories:

- "genuine" intuitive impressions
- "imagined" intuitive impressions
- "interference"

With feedback—which the exercises in this book provide—you will discover which of these tend to be accurate "hits" and which are off the mark.

A NOTE ABOUT THE PROGRESS YOU CAN EXPECT

Gaining conscious control over your intuition is like learning to ride a bicycle—it takes some practice to get the hang of things, but once you have the knack it's not difficult at all.

I say this because some beginning students experience frustration about now. Don't expect each exercise to go smoothly. You're tuning an instrument—your intuition—and you should expect some sour notes. They're all part of the process.

Response to **Exercise 14:** You were answering your Question 1.

- 13 -
INTUITION IS KNOWING WITHOUT
KNOWING *WHY* YOU KNOW

WHAT DO WE MEAN BY INTUITION?

We have been speaking a lot about intuition already without having defined exactly what it is. It's important that we do so now because the concept is used very loosely to mean many things.

For example, the word *intuitive* is often used as a synonym for *prophetic* or *subconscious* or *instinctive,* three words that have widely different meanings and connotations. It is often used these days to mean "easily understood," as when engineers speak of a computer's "intuitive interface."

≈≈≈

INTUITION IN ACTION
AN ANECDOTE

I remember many years ago a five-year-old girl was brought to me for a healing. Sara had encephalitis, had suffered a seizure at age two, and had been in a coma and catatonic ever since. When she came to me, she was stiff as a board and showed no response to anything. Her hands and jaws were clenched so tightly that I hoped she was beyond feeling. She was fed by a tube inserted directly into her stomach. The only thing this child did without assistance was breathe.

I remember her mother placing Sara on the couch for me to do a laying on of hands, and I thought to myself, "I can't do anything for this girl." I was so moved by the sight of this child and her devoted mother that I didn't know if this was a feeling or an intuition.

The mother's reason for bringing the girl to me at that particular time was that the doctors were insisting on putting her in an institution since the child couldn't "know or feel" anything anyway. She wanted to try every last thing before even considering such a move.

I gave the mother my usual lecture about how the laying on of hands often doesn't work, and that the doctors' opinion and her own good sense were the most important considerations in making any decision. Then, without much hope, I did a "healing."

While I was working, I saw terrible pictures in my head of a man's face bloodied, and then the child's face bloodied—first alternating, then transposed on each other. In my mind's eye, I tried to make the man's face go away and to see the child's face clearly. I felt the child wanting to follow the man, and I asked her, in my mind, to stay with me and her mother. While I was doing the healing, I felt very hopeful about this child's recovery, but once I opened my eyes and saw the unresponsive, spastic child before me, I knew I was wrong.

The mother called me a few days later to tell me that Sara had begun to lick her lips. It seemed to me like a very small improvement, but the mother was elated and wanted me to work with her more. She really believed that her child would get better, and I, although not wanting to encourage her unrealistic perceptions, felt that a few more sessions would help her make the decision to do as the doctors suggested and institutionalize the child.

I continued to work with Sara on a weekly basis, and she continued to improve. It was amazing to see, not only because I thought that the situation was hopeless but because of the way she healed, going over all the developmental steps a baby and young child learns in rapid motion. Learning to make sounds and then words and then sentences, learning to roll, then to sit, then to crawl, and finally to walk.

After I had known the mother and daughter for about six months, I asked where the father was. The mother told me that he had been shot in the head when Sara was one and a half and that he had died.

I still see this beautiful child occasionally. She is in school and doing well. I wonder whether the little girl sensed her father's manner of death and somehow replicated it in her own body, or whether it was just a coincidence that she became ill in the same area of the body where her father had been fatally wounded. I am grateful that I didn't go on my first "intuition" that she would not recover.

≈≈≈

INTUITION IS YOUR SIXTH SENSE

You use your five primary physical senses—touch, sight, smell, hearing, taste—to gather information about the world around you. As you hold this book in your hands and read it, you're gathering information through your senses. You feel the weight of the book, for example, and hear the pages when you turn them. Your eyes receive the light reflected off the page. The light goes through your lenses and stimulates the retinas, which in turn send messages along the optic nerves to your brain.

The key difference is that intuition perceives things *without reliance on senses.* Intuition is nothing more than a process of gaining information that does not rely on your senses, your memory, your experience, your feelings, or your other thought processes— though it does rely on these to *interpret* that information.

INTUITION DEFINED

We will define intuition concisely in the following way:

> *Intuition is a nonlinear, nonempirical process of gaining and interpreting information in response to questions.*

That's a mouthful, so let's examine this definition term by term to see what it means.

First: Intuition Is a Nonlinear Process

Deduction, a kind of formal reasoning, starts with premises and information, from which it draws conclusions and inferences. Intuition, on the other hand, does not proceed in "logical" steps.

Intuition does not reason, nor does it need to. Intuition simply knows. Instantly. Where reason plods, intuition proceeds in flashes. Intuition gets glimpses of reality in bits and pieces, usually as symbols. These symbols must then be interpreted and assembled for a coherent picture to emerge.

≋

INTUITION IN ACTION
A STUDENT'S ANECDOTE

At one time, I was thinking of buying a failing company. Their products didn't interest me, but their production setup did, although I didn't have a detailed vision of what I would do with it. I had seen Laura a few years before, when there was talk that the company I was then working for would be sold. She told me at that time that the company would be sold and to whom. She told me who would be fired and who would keep their jobs—and why. She outlined in great detail the objectives of the buyer, why they would make certain policy decisions, and how I should work around them. Using this information, I did not lose my job, although I later, as predicted, chose to leave.

Laura made me take copious notes on our session. And from time to time over the succeeding few years I reviewed them. She had accurately predicted events within the company and my life years before they happened.

I came to Laura the second time with a very precise list of questions. Together, she and I came up with a business plan for the company I was considering, which has been very successful. Laura foresaw problems in a publicity campaign for a product that hadn't yet been created. She provided valuable information about refining a product that hadn't yet been conceived! With her help, we also identified competitors that weren't even in the market yet, and we anticipated how they would compete.

I am an atheist and not a big believer in things that go bump in the night, but I do believe in using whatever works. I skipped the crisis of belief, although what Laura was able to see was unbelievable. Then she told me something that I found harder to believe than anything she had said before: She said that I could make the same kinds of predictions she made with the same degree of accuracy.

I asked her to come into my company and do a training. My staff was scarcely open-minded, but even the most skeptical among them had to admit that the results were astounding. Although I've found there are differing degrees of intuitive ability, my entire staff was capable of performing intuitively with some proficiency, and some were extraordinary. It was also helpful to identify the people who were especially talented intuitives and those were more thinking based.

I now use intuitive "brainstorming" in my company all the time. Intuitive information doesn't replace "hard facts"; it adds new facts by providing information beyond the reach of traditional methods, such as logic.

≈≈≈

Second: Intuition Gathers Information Through Nonempirical Means

Empirical means "based on experience or experiment." If I ask you whether you will go to your office tomorrow, the empirical approach would be to know that it's going to be a weekday and, barring a sudden illness or personal emergency, assume you'll be in the office. Intuition, however, does not need "data" to provide an answer. With intuition, you can even answer questions about topics you "know nothing about."

Having drawn these distinctions, I should say that the line between intuitive and empirical data is not always clear. Is a Native American's prediction of rain based on his set of data any less empirical than that of the ever-mistaken Channel 2 weatherman's prediction based on *his* data?

All we're talking about is information, which we receive in a variety of ways, according to what we have access to. In judging whether it will rain, the Native American uses different data from the meteorologist's, but so does the sea captain or arthritic. When we were a preverbal tribe, we probably used our intuition to interact with and access our environment to a far greater degree than we do now.

Intuitive information is nonempirical because you don't receive it through your senses. Once you receive an intuitive impression and use it to draw a conclusion, however, it becomes empirical.

When you pick up an intuitive image of a future event, your reasoning mind can use that image just as readily as it can any tangible image.

Third: Intuition Interprets Information

Intuition does not merely gather information, it interprets it. Indeed, intuitive impressions *must* be interpreted to be useful, in the same way that information in dreams must. The information we receive through our intuition is largely symbolic rather than literal. This inherent symbolism is true of all internal language (versus language we use to make ourselves understood to the world).

Many of us think of symbols or symbolic stories as a primitive or unclear or indirect form of communication. Why, we ask, can't our intuition speak to us more "clearly"?

Actually, symbols are a highly sophisticated form of communication. They convey a great deal of detail much more economically than do literal words. A writer uses allegory and symbolism as ways to provide the reader detail and information on many levels.

≈≈≈

INTUITION IN ACTION
A STUDENT'S ANECDOTE

I saw Laura after the death of my boyfriend. He had died under very mysterious circumstances from a pneumonia usually associated with AIDS. I was in such shock from the loss that it didn't occur to me to have him tested before the burial.

I lived the following few months in fear, preparing to die. I didn't start any new relationships or long-term projects. I spoke to no one about my fears and the manner of my boyfriend's death. When I arrived at Laura's office, the first thing she said to me was "You are perfectly healthy. Why are you living your life as a dying person?"

I didn't believe in intuitives, and I really had no idea what a reading was. I was so taken aback by the oddity of this little stranger, and by the blunt manner in which she made this accurate statement about something no one could have known, that I told her the whole story. She gave me the names of a therapist and a doctor. She said, "Call the therapist first and the doctor second, because positive or negative will be an adjustment."

I ignored her advice and called the doctor first, got tested, learned I was negative, and then spent the worst few months of my life, realizing that I had to keep living without Mark. About that time a depression started that I couldn't shake.

I didn't get in touch with Laura again for almost a year. I called her because in my notes from the session were some incredibly accurate details about a business move and partnership offer that had made no sense at the time of the reading but now had occurred just as she had foreseen. She even gave me the name of the city and the name of the partner. I couldn't understand how she could have known these things, and my curiosity overwhelmed my discomfort. So I called her.

I have, since that time, become a student of intuition, and I use it in every area of my life. It took an intuitive reading to get me to do what logic should have directed. See a doctor, get the facts, and deal with them.

I did eventually see a therapist to deal with the survival terror. I wish I had done so sooner. I wonder if Laura knew I was HIV negative before she sent me to be tested. She won't tell me and refused to tell me at the time, saying, "Even if I could, what purpose would it serve when, for two tubes of blood, you can get a concrete answer?" She insisted that she was not the correct professional to make a medical diagnosis, nor was she equipped to deal with the psychological implications of a diagnosis, and she steered me to two highly qualified people who were.

I wonder where my life would have gone if I had continued to live in the shadow of my fear that I was going to die soon.

≈≈≈

Fourth: Intuition Responds to Questions

Finally, you will notice from the definition that intuition must be "set in motion" by a question. The question focuses your intuition and tells you what you need to notice in the world around you.

Every second there are a million questions within you waiting to be answered, and a million answers in the process of formation.

Even a belief is a question at rest. All our senses respond to the questions our environment and our "body machine" pose—that's their job. Your rational mind's job is to interpret the information provided by these senses for more efficient survival. Your intuitive mind's job is to interpret these senses for the same purpose. In reawakening and noticing your intuitive mind at work, you will realize just how far-reaching your senses are.

Intuition responds to questions, even the ones we haven't consciously asked. Intuition functions to bring to consciousness that information which lies beyond what our rational minds perceive from our five senses: people we don't know, places we haven't been to or can't see, the future.

A FEW WORDS OF REASSURANCE

In this chapter we defined what we mean by intuition, but don't let definitions or explanations get in the way of what is a simple, human process. Remember, you are already intuitive.

- 14 -

INTUITION'S RELATIONSHIP TO OTHER "PSYCHIC" PHENOMENA

INTUITION IS NOT TELEPATHY

You will get a better understanding of intuition by comparing it with related phenomena with which it's often confused.

Intuition is often mislabeled a "psychic" ability. It's sometimes equated, for example, with reading people's minds, or telepathy. Telepathy, however, is only one small part of your intuitive self! You don't usually go to an intuitive to find out what you're thinking (though an intuitive can clarify what may be causing you confusion).

There is also a great deal of New Age talk these days of "mediums" or "channels." As I view them, mediums are people who talk to "spirits" or through whom "spirits" speak. Once you find a centered state from which you're open to receiving information, that same sensing and receiving can be used for a variety of purposes: telepathy, precognition, and healing as well as mediumship.

Mediumship is most useful when people lose someone close to them, and with whom they have to work out unresolved issues as part of their healing and grieving process. This is usually the only time I will practice mediumship, unless I receive a strong sense that a "spirit" wants to give a message that will really help a person in some way.

People always want to know how something works, believing that every result must be comprehensible and have a "logical" explanation. How mediumship works is a mystery. I don't think anybody really knows if it is the spirit actually speaking or an energy that has been left behind or an intuitive's ability to enter a state in which he or she has access to information about things we normally don't perceive, at least not consciously. (I can tell you from firsthand experience, however, that genuine mediumship does exist.)

DREAMS ARE NOT INTUITIVE

Many people place great importance on the signs and insights their dreams provide. More and more you hear people saying, "Well, I've had a dream and this is what happened and this is what that means to me." The mistake people make with their dreams is not realizing that dreams have meanings on multiple levels.

It is commonly thought that dreams can foretell the future. In fact, intuition is at work in such cases. Dreams are your psyche working out the unconscious conflicts and experiences of the day. In that "space," intuition can make use of the same symbolic language as dreams.

But receiving information through intuition is not at all the same as receiving it through your dreams. A key difference is that, whereas intuition is objective and often predictive, dreams are always subjective and descriptive.

It's generally accepted that dreams are figurative and symbolic rather than literal, and that their "meanings" must be interpreted to be fully understood. Notice that we receive the information in the dream state but we interpret that information during our normal waking state.

There are different types of dreams, of course. The content of dreams is a mixture of the day's events, memories, and feelings. The purpose dreams have in our psychological functioning is not fully understood, but they appear to operate as a kind of downloading system. Dreams focus our awareness on things we've noticed throughout the day but haven't noted. They bring up to "semiconsciousness" information necessary for our psychological well-being.

DREAMS AND INTUITION COMPARED

Dreams and intuition share a number of enlightening similarities as well as differences.

Generally speaking, both must be interpreted to be understood. Further, both provide information in one state that must be interpreted in our waking state. The logical filters that operate during our normal waking state inhibit the operation of dreaming as well as intuition. Finally, both use what is available to us to express information. If you're not a mathematician or scientist, it is highly unlikely that you will either dream or intuit equations!

On the other hand, dreams generally present information in the form of a story line, whereas intuitive information is often fragmentary. Also, in dreams you are the central character. When receiving intuitive information, you are only rarely a character.

- 15 -

FINDING YOUR INTUITIVE STATE

YOU DON'T NEED TO BECOME A YOGI OR A ZEN MONK

The popular image of a practicing intuitive ("psychic" or "medium" in pop vernacular) doing a reading is an eccentric individual in some altered state of consciousness. Though that may be Hollywood's idea, intuition is a quite ordinary state of consciousness. Again, intuition requires nothing more than a slight shift in attention.

Having said that, intuition is not something vague but a specific physical state in which you're open to intuitive information. By *physical state* I am not referring to distinctions between alpha and theta brainwaves, or those between right- and left-brain thought processes. Nor does being open mean becoming "empty" in any mystical sense. We are more aware in both our dream state and an intuitive state because our normal, waking cognitive "filters" are down. As we discussed, we must wake up from dreams in order to make sense of them. The same applies to intuition: we must "wake up" and use our rational mind to make sense of our impressions.

The intuitive state is a state of waiting—not of expectation but simply of patient waiting. You will reach the intuitive state easily with practice.

INTUITION IN ACTION
A STUDENT'S ANECDOTE

The film started out badly. The writers had been fighting with the producer from the beginning. By the end of the first week, we were already on our second director. Instead of the typical camaraderie on film sets, nobody could agree on anything. Between vegetarian, kosher, and meat and potatoes, we couldn't even go out to the same restaurant for dinner. I had a major role in the film, and I had worked hard on my character. I wanted the film to be a success.

At the end of the second week of shooting, I had just finished a scene with the male lead. He was as frustrated as I was. Unlike me, however, he was not giving much to the film because of his frustration. Neither, I realized, were many of the other members of the cast and crew.

I finally lost my patience. I went to my trailer, slammed some doors to vent, and sat down to get ahold of myself. I started to space out a little. All of a sudden I got a very strong image of guys joking and laughing, a kind of male-bonding kidding around. I started laughing. I realized that almost everyone on the film was a guy—and a "guy's guy" to boot. I intuitively realized at that moment that the key was to goad them into being good guys—guys instead of beasts.

That afternoon on the set I started cracking jokes, and everyone joined in. Even the guys who had set themselves apart were too "guy" not to respond to a good joke. I think it's a male code or something.

The film, among those of us who worked on it, is remembered for its laughter and camaraderie, and we all ended up doing a great job and using the initial tension in a creative way. Now when I need to problem-solve and the information eludes me (although I still slam some doors), I sit down, take a deep breath, and wait for the answer to arrive.

≈≈≈

WHAT IS THE INTUITIVE STATE?

In "normal functioning," logic filters our feelings, emotions, and even intuitions. In the intuitive state, intuition becomes the precursor to all the other senses.

When we say, for example, that someone is an emotional person, we mean that the basis for all his or her other functions—reason, choice making, reaction, physical sensation—is triggered by or based on that person's emotionality, while the people we call rational are those who base all their responses on analysis and judgment.

HOW DOES YOUR INTUITIVE STATE FEEL?

By now you may have realized that, every time you do an exercise in this book, you are giving your unconscious a cue it uses to shift into an intuitive state. Just as Pavlov trained his dogs through repetition, you are conditioning your subconscious to respond to the cues you give it when preparing to function "intuitively," even though you will not be aware of all the preparation your subconscious does to access intuition.

Take a moment to notice how you feel when you are in an intuitive state. Do you sense any changes in your perception of your physical body? Do you feel lighter? Heavier? Warmer? Cooler?

Is your thinking quicker or slower? Does your perception of the sounds around you change? Is your breathing different? Do you feel different emotionally than when you are in your "normal" state? Does the focus of your attention feel different to you? Do things look different to you? Is your visual focus sharper or more diffuse?

This awareness will be important in the reverse when you finish a reading and do grounding exercises to get back to a "normal" or, more aptly, your natural state of consciousness, where you feel most at home. Even your "natural" cognitive state may change as you do the exercises in this book, just as going through therapy changes the normal state of your consciousness. Not only the information you receive from your readings but the practice of intuitive receptivity in and of itself may affect who you are.

RECOGNIZING THE INTUITIVE STATE: HOW DO YOU KNOW WHETHER YOU'RE BEING INTUITIVE?

One of the most common questions students of intuition have asked me over the years is "How can I be sure I'm intuiting and not projecting my fears or hopes?" In other words, "How can I tell when a hunch is intuitive (that is, valid) and not something simply made up or a random lucky guess?"

My standard response is "You *don't* know." I'm not being facetious; that's the whole challenge of using intuition.

Having said that, one obvious way of knowing whether you've been using your intuition is the extent to which the impressions you receive during a reading are confirmed by experience.

Let's say you get a sense that the price of a certain stock will rise in the next month. If it doesn't, your "sense" was a feeling or an opinion—or a hope! If the stock does rise, it is likely you had an intuitive hit. Of course, it may have been a "lucky guess." Over time, however, and a large number of such predictions, good and bad luck tend to cancel each other, and you'll learn to recognize when you're on the right track.

Practice applying your intuition often. Each time you consciously access your intuition, get feedback by comparing the impressions you receive with "reality." In a very short time you will learn to distinguish a genuine intuitive impression from your feelings or projections, particularly your hopes and fears.

Here are other indicators of the intuitive to keep in mind:

- **Intuition—like your emotions—is more likely to express itself through metaphors and symbols than is the reasoning mind.**
- **Intuition is detached from its perceptions.** Searching intuitively is being open to perception without expectation. There is no feeling attached to it. A sure sign of your shifting from intuiting to reasoning, then, is when your internal dialogue begins eliciting emotions such as fear or anger in response to a question. Another sign is when your internal dialogue begins to use words like *should.*
- Finally, **intuition perceives the world in wholes (albeit fragmentary wholes) rather than parts to be analyzed.** Intuitive impressions rarely follow one another in "logical" fashion. If you find yourself thinking, "If this happens, then that would likely happen," you are reasoning rather than intuiting.

USING SIGNPOSTS TO VERIFY INTUITIVE IMPRESSIONS

There's a logic to knowing, and ways or signposts we can use to see whether our normal thought processes "make sense." These might include our experiences, or the laws of logic, or the consistency and coherence of our premises and conclusions.

For that matter, even dreams have a kind of logic and internal consistency. With intuition, though, you're flying blind, since you don't have any such internal or external "checks."

You can, however, consciously supply checks by seeking what I call signposts. If, for example, you get an impression of marriage between two people next May, you could ask your intuition where each person will be living next summer. If you get an impression of different states, you have a signpost that tells you your earlier impression of marriage may have been mistaken.

We'll talk more about signposts later. Even with them, however, you can never be completely sure. I can reassure you that, with practice and continual feedback, you will learn to distinguish whether your internal state indicates genuine intuition or not.

INTUITION AND YOUR UNCONSCIOUS

Although the intuitive self often borrows the language of the unconscious to describe itself, the unconscious and the place from which we receive intuitive data are actually different. Just as we must often describe the nonspecific, nonverbal condition of feeling through the language of our beliefs or the postures and expressions of our faces and bodies, our intuitive perceptions must borrow a language that is available to our conscious minds.

OPENING UP

Each person must find his or her own way to get in touch with the intuitive state. It helps to relax, by finding a comfortable seat and taking several deep breaths. An image many of my students find helpful is the tops of their heads opening up to receive intuitive information. With practice you will undoubtedly find an image or approach that works well for you.

INTUITION IS A HIGHLY RIGOROUS PROCESS

Intuition involves more than simply "going with your gut" or "trusting your hunches." A common misconception about intuition is that it means not having to think about things. Even the expression "going with your gut" implies that intuition does not take place in the head.

Simply not thinking logically, however, does not mean you're being intuitive. In fact, while using intuition you are actively observing and recording your impressions, interpreting them, and finally integrating them with your other mental processes.

Now, as we have repeatedly discussed, you are already intuitive. So the highly rigorous process I just referred to is something you do all the time, albeit imperfectly. Again, our aim is to give you conscious control over your intuitive faculty.

INTUITION PROCEEDS IN TWO STEPS

Intuition, then, is about receiving and interpreting information. As you gain control over your intuition, it's important to keep these two steps distinct.

The first step is receiving intuitive data in response to a question. Intuitive information usually presents itself as symbols. This step is nonlinear.

The second step is both linear and nonlinear. At this stage you're both interpreting, or translating, the symbols and piecing them together. It's linear in the sense that you use your logical mind to fill in and make sense of the gaps.

It's in the translation process that useful and applicable information is created. I use the word *translation* because intuitive data are often received in the symbolic language of the unconscious, and the practitioner then has to find the meaning or significance of the "messages."

You will learn to apply a logical, problem-solving process to assemble intuitive information into a useful form. Sometimes information comes as a straight answer, and then you have to open to more impressions to verify the answer. Often the initial answer comes in the form of a series of data received through different senses that you must synthesize into an answer. This process becomes instantaneous once you're a practiced intuitive, but initially this is where most people make their mistakes.

A BRIEF SUMMARY

This chapter was chock-full of information, so a recap is in order. The intuitive state is simply one in which you gather information without relying on your senses or mental processes. Instead of blindly relying on this intuitive information, you must then assemble, verify, and interpret it in a rigorous fashion. In that sense intuition is a two-step process, not unlike that of first having dreams and then waking up to interpret them.

16

IN THE BEGINNING WAS THE QUESTION

LIFE IS CONTINUALLY SEEKING ANSWERS

What you notice in the world about you, through your intellect and memory as well as your intuition, is a response to questions. Everything you do consists of answering questions, from something as mundane as "What's for dinner?" through more important matters like "Who should I marry?" and "Is this the right career for me?" all the way up to transcendent questions, such as "Why am I here?" and "What does it all mean?"

It's these questions that lend life its drama. And what makes your life different from mine is largely the questions we ask ourselves. Indeed, the important thing in life is knowing what questions we should be asking.

INTUITION IS GOAL DIRECTED

Keep in mind that intuition always activates in response to a question and presents you with information—images, sensations, impressions, or symbols. To understand intuitive data, you must become aware of the questions you consciously—or unconsciously—ask.

The trick is that we are not conscious of all the questions we ask. Indeed, we often subconsciously give our intuition conflicting signals ("I want a raise, yet I don't want the added responsibility"; "I want love, but then I'm afraid of losing it"). In a real sense this is a book about learning to notice the answers to questions you're not conscious of asking. The problem with our unconscious, of course, is that it really *is* unconscious!

INTUITION SIMPLY RESPONDS TO QUESTIONS

One block many students of intuition experience is the pressure of finding the "right" answer. After years of schooling, we have all been conditioned to fear questions.

It's more helpful to think of your task as simply reporting the "sense" and impressions you get *in response* to a question. For example, if I were to ask you whether there would be a drought in the Midwest next summer, you might suddenly become more aware of the flashes of light behind your eyelids. When tuning in to this, you might get a sense of lightning, and then storms, and then a bathtub that overflowed when you were six years old, and all the trouble that got you into, even though it soon blew over.

These sensations are your intuitive responses to the question. The important thing when doing a reading is to assume that all your thoughts, senses, feelings, and memories are providing you with information about the question you are asking. Don't discount or dismiss anything—however seemingly irrelevant.

Of course, there is more to intuition than simply reporting your impressions—you must interpret them. For the moment, though, view your task as simply reporting impressions.

INTUITION ESTABLISHES A DIALOGUE WITH THE WORLD

In traditional Western thought, answers follow questions. With intuition, questions follow answers. One question will lead to one or more impressions, which will suggest other images and other questions, which will in turn suggest yet other questions—even ones you haven't thought to ask.

For example, if someone asks you when a partner will propose marriage, you might get an image of a lake. Other questions arise: What time of year is it? What time of day?

Often a question that you don't receive an answer to from one direction can be successfully approached from a different one. If you don't get an impression of the time of year in response to that question, ask another: What will the person be wearing when he proposes marriage? Will this occur before the Fourth of July? Will this occur after Easter? And so on.

ALLOW ONE IMPRESSION TO SUGGEST OTHERS, LIKE DOMINOES

In a sense, no question can be asked without raising still other questions. Impressions and questions follow one another. But they do so in a nonlinear fashion rather than a rigid sequence (which would suggest that your reasoning—as opposed to your intuitive—mind was at work).

For example, you might get an intuitive image of a kitchen, then a sense of a knife, and then a sense of being afraid. Notice the difference between that sequence and a more logical one, which might have moved from the image of a kitchen to cooking to eating breakfast.

THE "CREATIVE" PART OF INTUITION

It's not an accident that dreams present themselves to us as stories. The inherent structure of stories is probably "hardwired" into human brains, and it may even have something to do with the experience of consciousness itself. As I mentioned earlier, however, one difference between dreams and intuition is the fragmentary nature of intuitive impressions. One impression often seems to follow another like a non sequitur. We have to do a little nudging to get them to weave a story that begins to "make sense."

You'll notice that in many of the previous exercises your initial perceptions in response to a question led to other perceptions. Learn to "follow" your perceptions without "forcing" them.

Don't worry if creating a story seems like you're "making something up." As children we are continually admonished to "tell the truth" and not to "make things up." But we must often make things up *in order* to tell the truth. We'll be discussing this in more detail shortly. For now, the following exercise will help you get back in touch with a natural part of your childhood self.

EXERCISE 15
ALLOWING IMPRESSIONS TO CREATE A STORY

The question you will be responding to in this exercise appears at the bottom of page 104. Take a long, deep breath and allow yourself to get a visual image. If you can't see anything, pretend you're seeing something, and report what you are "seeing."

Now allow that image to make up a story about itself. Record the story as you follow the narrative intuitively.

You don't have to make an effort. Simply allow the image to lead you. Continue for a few minutes, until the story naturally breaks off.

When you're done, ask yourself the following questions about your story:

- What did the original image remind you of?
- How did the final image or story compare with the initial one?
- Was there a lot of "movement" or change between the initial image and the final one?
- What qualities describe that movement?

Don't be confused if your imagery changes according to the experiences of a particular day or state of mind. Your unconscious will use whatever is most readily available to it to display the correct information.

When you've completed this exercise, turn to page 104 to see the question you were answering. Remember to use your intuition notebook.

A BRIEF REFLECTION ON THE EXERCISE

Everything in life changes or is perceived as changing. What do you know about the direction and "energy" of your question now that you've completed this exercise? Does your "story" remind you of any other patterns or situations in your life?

ONE STUDENT'S READING

The following reading was done by a student who had been estranged from his brother for a number of years. The question this exercise referred to for him was "Will my brother and I resolve our differences?"

A ghoulish face with scary white hair, but when I look more closely I see it is the face of someone I love and I am grateful at having rediscovered. I cannot join this person, and this person cannot join me, but we can make contact and create a relationship, each from our own hemisphere.

Here's how he interpreted his reading once he saw the question:

The original image reminded me of something from the classic horror movie *Night of the Living Dead.* In the final image I recognized the positive and deep connection the original image had to me, and my desire and ability to dialogue with it. There was a lot of internal movement from the first image to the final one, but the external movement was blocked. The communication held the promise of the final image's moving forward, having gained something from the original one. I also felt that the final image could return to the original image for counsel. It reminds me of the saying "The child is father of the man." The qualities describing the movement are insight, the ability to look deeper and find meaning, the ability to recognize the beauty in everything, and the ability to leave a premise and then return.

I would say that my brother and I will resolve our differences by respecting the fact that we will not share a point of view. I get the sense this conflict might ultimately be good for the evolution of our relationship. We are still arguing about the same things we did when we were kids. Maybe we need to form a more adult bond and allow it to gain strength from the history we have together, without expecting the same kinds of compromises in viewpoint we were able to reach as children. The ghoulish face reminds me that

I tend to make my brother either good when we are in agreement or bad when we aren't. I guess I'm no longer the big brother who can expect to impose agreement on his younger sibling.

HELPFUL HINT

A reading can provide more information than the question asked. Look for the layers of meaning available to you when doing your interpretation.

17

YOUR FIRST SOLO READING

THROWING YOURSELF IN AT THE DEEP END

Learning how to use your intuition is not like learning how to play the piano, requiring weeks of practice before you can bang out a simple tune. There is no better way consciously to experience your intuition than to jump right in and give a reading.

The earlier exercises were like riding a bicycle with training wheels. This one is the real thing.

Remember, this is a practical book. It's time now for you to see what it feels like to experience intuition. The following exercise is one I use in my workshops. It forces you to give an intuitive as opposed to linear response to questions by restricting your use of empirical data. In later chapters you'll learn more formal ways of accessing and interpreting intuitive data. But the results of even this simple introductory exercise may astonish you.

Remember, too, you are already intuitive. You just need to get back in touch with that part of yourself. Trust me: You will amaze yourself with your intuitive abilities, even at this early stage.

A DAY AT THE RACES

The first time I ever went to the racetrack, I took twenty dollars to bet. I knew absolutely nothing about picking horses and was simply tagging along with an expert "handicapper." He knew the times on all the horses and how they ran under which conditions. He was convinced that he made his choices based on hard data derived from the history of the horses' performance.

We arrived at the track just in time for the third race. We got in a long line at the teller's window, and my friend began to peruse the racing form. In my mind's eye I saw a young girl running through a field of green. As my friend was quickly going over the "facts" he knew about each horse in the field, I saw in the race a horse called Clover Miss and placed a ten-dollar bet. My friend, the expert handicapper, was amused by my "subjective" approach and teased me about wagering half my money on such a "long shot."

Needless to say, Clover Miss won by several lengths.

That day began a profitable association I have enjoyed with racetracks. Though I am by no means always correct, I do generally earn a comfortable return on my capital.

The following exercise will demonstrate that you, too, can predict the winners of horse races!

A FOUR-PART EXERCISE

I'll walk you through this reading. I've divided the exercise into four parts so that we can discuss them. As you gain experience giving readings, however, these parts will blend seamlessly. Proceed through all four parts in this exercise without taking a break, which might interfere with your level of concentration.

Your goal is to tell me as much as possible the name of the horse I have selected that wins a race. You will find the names of the nine horses in this race in the actual exercise, and the name of the winner appears at the bottom of page 110.

Since you will not be given clues or information of any kind, you'll be forced to rely on your intuition. Trust that your intuitive sense has access to anything you would like to know about the name of this horse.

Don't cheat. I say this because I know you'll be tempted. But don't peek at the answer until you've completed the exercise.

HERE'S WHAT YOU'LL NEED

As always, you'll need something to write with, your intuition notebook, and your tape recorder. Set aside at least fifteen uninterrupted minutes for this exercise. It's important that you not feel rushed in any way. Take the phone receiver off the hook or turn off the ringer. If you have an answering machine, turn down the volume so any incoming messages will not distract you.

The final thing you need is a willingness to work as if you already know how to do something that you *do* already know how to do—indeed already have done in many exercises.

≈

EXERCISE 16
GOING TO THE RACES

You will shortly see a list of the names of nine thoroughbred horses in a race. The winner of the race is listed at the bottom of page 110.

Which horse won the race? You will not be given any clues on which to base your information other than those provided by your intuitive impressions.

Again, you'll find it helpful to use a tape recorder to record your responses as you do your reading. If you don't have a recorder handy, enlist a friend who can scribble fast to keep up with you. If neither is available, you can jot down your responses yourself.

STEP 1: GETTING CENTERED

Take a long, deep breath, and as you exhale give yourself the suggestion that any thoughts, pictures, feelings, sounds, or sensations you'll have in the next few minutes will contain information about the name of the winner of the race you've chosen.

Notice that the question asks for the *name* of the horse, not the *horse* itself. As we discussed earlier, the precise wording of the question is crucial. If you ask yourself "about the horse" rather than for its name, you might receive intuitive impressions describing its mane or its running style!

STEP 2: REPORTING YOUR INITIAL IMPRESSIONS

Take another long, deep breath and allow your body to relax completely. Begin speaking, and either record or have your friend transcribe any thoughts, feelings, memories, images, or other impressions the name of the winner evokes. Write everything down, even what you may consider mental interference.

Again, take a deep breath and allow your unconscious to give you symbols, letters, names, feelings, or explanations of the name of the horse who will win this race.

There are no right or wrong answers. Allow the name of the horse I selected as the winner to come to you without *trying*. If you feel "blocked," take a deep breath and continue.

You may speak for as long as you wish. Students speak on average for about thirty seconds, some more, some less. At some point the impressions will taper off, forming a natural break, at which you can stop.

At this step, do *not* analyze or interpret your impressions. For example, if you receive an impression of the sun, don't say, "I get an impression of the sun. That must mean you're in a warm place. . . ." You'll be interpreting your impressions in the next step.

Allow your impressions to tell you about the name of the winner. Don't, however, expect or force your impressions to be all in terms of horses or even names. It's quite possible to give a highly accurate intuitive reading without getting any impressions of horses.

Reporting intuitive impressions is like playing charades. If you've never played this classic game, the object is to give clues to your partner about something, typically the name of a movie or a book or a famous person, without mentioning any names. All your clues must be indirect and acted out. Likewise, here you're looking not for literal details but for *clues*, a sense of the winning horse I selected.

STEP 3: REVIEWING YOUR IMPRESSIONS FOR THEMES

When you've finished reporting your initial impressions, play them back or look over what your friend has transcribed for you. Do any themes stand out? Any predominant letters? Do you get a sense of colors? Are there descriptive words of any kind?

Report your initial impressions.

STEP 4: LOOKING OVER YOUR CHOICES

Now that you've reported your intuitive impressions, look at the names of the horses for the race.

1. Rose Red
2. Man o' War
3. Rolling Thunder
4. Snow White
5. Field of Dreams
6. Indian Path
7. Dancing Dan
8. Jingle Bells
9. Little Mermaid

Is there a name that matches your clues? Which of the names feels like it most fits with what you've written?

Don't expect an exact match between your clues. Many students pick the name of the winner although their clues don't seem to have anything to do with the horse they select.

Write your first choice. Remember to use your intuition notebook.

≈≈≈

THAT'S ALL THERE IS TO IT

You've just completed your first solo reading. In the next chapter we'll review your intuitive impressions. If you can't take the suspense, turn now to page 110 to see if you identified the horse I selected. I also, as in a real race, selected the second and third—or place and show—horses' names. Compare your results against all three possibilities. Even if you picked third place, you're doing well.

- 18 -

REVIEWING YOUR FIRST SOLO READING

AND THE WINNER BY A NOSE IS . . .

If you haven't already done so, look at the answer at the bottom of this page. Compare your intuitive impressions with the names of the first three winners listed under this exercise. Almost all those who do this exercise are startled by how accurate their intuitions were, despite knowing absolutely nothing about the entrants I picked. Most students are also entertained as well as surprised by the way their personal biases, predilections, and psychology are revealed in their readings. I'm sure you will be, too.

NO READING IS PERFECT

If your responses seemed off the mark, don't be discouraged. You're just beginning to get in touch with your intuition. This was your first reading, and it often takes practice to get the hang of your intuitive style.

Did you notice any difference in the way you received your "hits" and your "misses"? Were your "genuine" intuitive impressions any more accurate than your "imagined" ones? Most people are astonished to discover that most of their impressions were on the mark, even those they assumed they had "just made up."

Response to **Exercise 16:** The horses finished in the following order: Indian Path, Dancing Dan, Little Mermaid.

I'm willing to bet, moreover, that your responses were closer to the mark than you realize. To demonstrate that, since I don't have your reading in front of me, let's analyze two readings. I'll present them here side by side to show you how parallel they are and how they diverge. (I recorded my impressions before I looked at the names I'd chosen.)

One Student's Impressions	**My Impressions**
It has a kind of creamy brown color. The name will have something to do with the elements, the elements and a color—such as blue air. I'm also getting something about water, something about sunset. That kind of cream, cloudy color, that's very strong.	The first thing I get is a sense of deep blue. I'm seeing little bells on a rope. And an *m*—like *mighty.* Something that has two. Not the number 2, but mirror images of each other. And a feather.

Interestingly, we both picked up the color blue, although that seemed to have nothing to do with the winning horse. Again, intuitive information doesn't always make sense.

I am not embarrassed to admit that my student picked the correct horse while I picked Rolling Thunder. She said she selected Indian Path based on the creamy brown color, which she associated with Indians.

When I review my responses, it appears I was picking up a sense of many of the horses. "Deep blue" points to Little Mermaid. "Little bells on a rope" seems to point to Jingle Bells. The "*m* for *mighty*" seems to point to Man o' War. "Mirror images" may refer to Dancing Dan. If I had focused more on the feather, I might have selected Indian Path. Frankly, I can't say why I selected Rolling Thunder based on my clues.

LOOKING FOR FEEDBACK

As you begin to get a sense of your intuitive style, look over the *type* of information you received. Did you receive primarily letters or complete words? Which sense was most dominant?

Also, how did you interpret (or, in my case, misinterpret) your impressions? I may have been confused by getting a sense of more than one horse. Perhaps I should have focused on this and asked myself some clarifying questions as signposts. You will recall we discussed this in Chapter 15.

BY THE WAY, BEFORE YOU RUSH OFF TO THE TRACK

Don't actually place bets on the horses you choose until you gain some proficiency. Placing a bet brings into play a lot of unconscious "stuff" (fear of failure, fear of success, greed), that may impede the free flow of intuitive information.

This exercise is a fun—and potentially profitable—way to practice the application of your intuition about a concrete event in a controlled way. It also gives immediate feedback on the accuracy of your intuitive impressions and interpretations.

When you practice this with a racing form or the sports section of your local paper, you'll need to be specific. Begin by picking the track you'll be working with, then pick the race.

- 19 -

INTUITION CAN TELL YOU
ABOUT *ANYTHING* YOU
WANT TO KNOW

INTUITIVE INFORMATION IS OBJECTIVELY VALID

Perhaps because intuition speaks to us through the language of symbols, gives us only fragments of reality, and proceeds in a non-linear fashion, it's usually dismissed as "subjective." In point of fact, the practicing intuitive insists on external feedback and verification just as rigorously as does the scientist applying the "scientific method."

Even Einstein, surely one of the towering intellects of modern times, admitted that scientific truth is revealed first through intuition, and only later verified by logic. How does the individual, confronted by the virtually infinite data available, select the most promising course of action? Intuition initially guides the scientist creating a hypothesis, the detective searching for clues, and the doctor piecing together a diagnosis.

≈

INTUITION IN ACTION
A STUDENT'S ANECDOTE

I began studying intuition ten years ago. At that point, I was a young woman married to a very successful older man who owned a small real estate business. I was not ready to have children, there was help to do the housekeeping and cooking, and I was tired of shopping. I was getting bored and increasingly depressed. I found some volunteer work and took a class in intuition that met once a month.

At the first class we did "general" readings, in which we each held an object belonging to another person and "made up" a story about the person's life.

The student who had my object told a version of the classic prince and the pauper story in which two young boys from "opposite sides of the track" trade places because of their uncanny resemblance. Although each believes the other has the better life, they soon miss their former worlds.

Here the student took poetic license by substituting girls for the two boys and spoke about how the pauper had always been an important part of her family because of her ability to pull them through difficult times and that now the pauper didn't feel part of any family at all, because she could give her parents money to solve their problems and her husband's "kingdom" could run perfectly well without her.

We had all been given code names to attach to our objects so no one would know who he or she was reading; the information would remain private for the person receiving the reading. I was grateful for what I had first considered a ridiculous exercise in cloak and dagger. I felt very exposed by the reading I had received.

I left this first class feeling extremely lonely. I didn't even remember the reading I had given for another student.

I continued to attend the workshops over the next year, and I began to look forward to them as I gained confidence in my intuitive ability and was sought out by other students to give readings. Sometimes when my husband was speaking about a business transaction, I would give him my impressions, and he was so happy I had found a way to occupy my time that he would listen.

As the months passed, my husband and I began to realize that my insights were valuable, and increasingly he would bring his business problems to me. Over the years my intuitive insights have become part of all the strategic decisions our company makes. I teach every person we hire how to integrate intuition into his or her decision-making process.

INTUITIVE INFORMATION IS *ALWAYS* VALID

The most common fallacy concerning intuition is that the *process* is somehow always right. Remember, however, that it's a two-part process: receiving and interpreting. Although the *information* we receive intuitively is always valid, we are human interpreters of this data. And when we assemble and translate intuitive information, it becomes subject to human error.

INTUITION KNOWS NO LIMITS

Unlike our physical senses or our reasoning abilities, intuition is limited by neither space nor time. Your intuition can tell you about things that have yet to happen, things you've never seen, in places you've never been. In that sense, intuition is an "idiot's art." It can be applied to anything, without the intuiter having any prior knowledge of the subject. Intuition does not require that you "know" anything about the subject that you're reading. It doesn't even require that you *understand* the impressions you're receiving!

Let's say an automobile mechanic comes to you for a reading. Something is wrong with a car, and he can't put his finger on the problem. Even though you may have no idea about the structure or workings of a car, you simply describe the feelings, pictures, and words that come to you as information about the dysfunction. The mechanic can then interpret your symbols and determine which parts of the car they represent.

WHY I'M NOT PERFECT!

As a practicing intuitive, I am frequently asked, "If you're so intuitive, why don't you have all the answers?" I don't have all the answers because I don't have all the questions. This is particularly the case when the intuitive information received is as simple as a yes or no, or a name. Without more context in which to interpret the intuitive information, the practitioner has to come up with a deductive process by which to verify that the question she thinks was asked is indeed the question that she's answering.

Whereas empirical decision making requires the most extensive knowledge available on a given topic, intuition requires only a question. In fact, the more you know or the more strongly you are emotionally attached to a particular outcome, the more your feelings interfere with both the receiving and the interpreting of intuitive data. This is one reason that it's easier to be clear in your intuitive readings of others than it is when reading yourself.

DEVIL'S ADVOCATE

Wait a second! If my intuition is not limited by any boundaries, then aren't you saying I know the answer to any question?

That is *exactly* what I am saying. Or rather, more precisely, I am saying that through your intuition you have *access* to all the answers. That's not quite the same thing as knowing everything, however. The trick is knowing the right questions to ask!

If your rational mind has trouble accepting the premise that your intuition can answer any question you put to it, try the following suggestion. *Pretend* that it can. In other words, *act* as if your intuitive impressions are the correct answers to the questions you consciously—or unconsciously—pose to your intuition. I promise you that in time you'll no longer need to pretend; the validating feedback you receive will confirm your trust.

- 20 -
Understanding Your
Unique Intuitive Vocabulary

To Make Sense, Intuitive Impressions Must Be Translated and Interpreted

A common misconception is that intuition speaks to us in complete, grammatically correct sentences or in images of filmlike clarity. The cliché image of intuition is usually the mother who suddenly senses that her young son has fallen off a swing in the schoolyard. Moments later she receives a phone call from the school confirming her fears.

Such a high degree of correspondence between intuitive impressions and what actually occurred is extraordinarily rare. One reason most people are out of touch with their intuition is that they expect a largely symbolic process to be this literal. In fact, as you may already have discovered, intuition communicates indirectly, in fragments and through symbols. Much of this translating process takes place unconsciously.

How literal your intuitive impressions are depends on which of the three primary intuitive modes you are accessing:

- *Clairvoyance* (clear seeing) is often literal, with little or no translation necessary.
- *Clairsentience* (clear sensing) is often highly figurative.
- *Clairaudience* (clear hearing) often seems literal. Here the translation process can be so instantaneous that what you're conscious of is a literal word or even sentence.

As a beginning intuitive, you'll find that the translation process will probably remain conscious for some time, but as you gain practice and experience, it will become virtually instantaneous. The same learning curve occurs when we study a new language. In the early stages there is a lot of conscious translating, but after a while we learn to think and express ourselves in the new language.

Although intuitive information is often received very clearly, it just as frequently comes in fragmentary voices and images and feelings. These bits and pieces must then be assembled by the practitioner to make sense. This is an intricate process, in which there is much room for error. The language of intuition is not always as clear as a yes or no; it is delivered in a mélange of symbol, sound, and feeling that then has to be interpreted and integrated by the rational, conscious mind.

Let's say that in response to several questions you got a very strong impression of an old car your father used to have. This may have been your intuition's way of telling you about a person named Ford. To someone else, of course, an old car might have meant something completely different.

A SIMPLE EXAMPLE

To help you appreciate the problems that can quickly arise when translating even the simplest intuitive information, consider what it might mean were you to get a sense of the sound of the letter *c*.

This could mean literally the letter *c*. It could also, however, mean any one of the following:

- the sea (a homonym)
- the Spanish word for *yes* (another homonym)
- a word beginning with the letter *c*
- something shaped like the letter *c*

Now, we can and should seek signposts to verify which of these meanings is correct, but I think this example makes clear that receiving impressions is only the first step in applying intuition to gain useful information.

The next step is to develop a logical, problem-solving process so that you can assemble the information you've received. Sometimes information comes in the form of a straight answer. You must then remain open to more impressions to verify that answer. But often the initial intuitive clue comes in the form of a series of data received through different senses that you must then synthesize into an answer. Initially this is the step where most people make their mistakes.

ONLY YOU CAN INTERPRET YOUR SYMBOLS

What is your symbol for pregnancy? One of my male students was highly accurate in intuiting upcoming pregnancies. His symbol? A window. Now I doubt very much that your symbol for pregnancy is a window; in fact, a window might have a completely different meaning for you.

Indeed, the same symbol can have completely *opposite* meanings for two persons. City girl that I am, the image of being alone in a rowboat on a moonlit lake would indicate danger to me. To someone raised in the country, this might be an image for peace, or romance.

What's more, the same symbol can have different meanings depending on the context. The color red, for example, can mean blood and death in one context and love in another.

WHY SYMBOL DICTIONARIES DON'T WORK, AND WHY YOU MUST COMPILE YOUR OWN

There is a fatal flaw in dictionaries of symbols with titles like *How to Interpret Your Dreams* or *The Meaning of Symbols.* Although there are archetypal images that are fairly common, the most powerful images, including the most powerful interpretations, are ones we form ourselves.

One of the first steps in developing intuition is to learn your own symbolic language. With practice you'll learn that certain symbols or impressions are, for you, highly reliable signs for certain things.

You may have found that the image of the sun is invariably a definite yes. Or that when the picture of your Uncle Joe appears, you know the subject of the reading is a sneaky, no-good bum.

As you do more and more readings, you'll find that you have a unique intuitive vocabulary, which is remarkably consistent and literal in its meanings. In daily life, intuitive awareness like this can provide useful insights. You may be introduced to someone who for some reason reminds you of your Uncle Joe. Your intuition has just given you a valuable clue about this person's trustworthiness.

Notice the images that come up for you and the events and emotions surrounding them. Note them in your intuition notebook. Make this a lifelong process.

≈≈≈

EXERCISE 17
GETTING IN TOUCH WITH YOUR INTUITIVE VOCABULARY

You can question yourself to find some of your sensory symbols. Report your responses to the following questions:

- How do you feel when someone tells you no?
- How do you feel when you are happy?
- What for you is a positive visual image? A negative one?
- What smell do you find distasteful? Which one do you find pleasing?

Remember to label this Exercise 17 in your intuition notebook.

≈≈≈

- 21 -

GIVING YOUR READINGS
A FRAMEWORK

SOME STRUCTURE HELPS

Before you gain mastery over your intuitive process, it's good to have a "structure" in which to place your intuitive impressions. The following exercise helps give boundaries and an organized sense of consecutive time progression to your intuitive impressions in response to a question.

The form I have chosen is a square. There is nothing special about this figure. I chose it simply because it's easy to visualize. If you have trouble visualizing one, draw a square on a piece of paper.

In each corner of the square, a scene is taking place. Begin in the lower-right-hand corner, which we will refer to as Corner 1 (you don't need to remember this—your unconscious will). This corner depicts what is happening now in reference to a question. Going clockwise to Corner 2, you'll find what will happen in reference to the question. Continuing around to the upper-left corner (3), you will see what is going to evolve from the previous scene. Finally, in Corner 4, you'll find how everything will change you or the subject of your question.

Here is a summary of the square's corners. Again, trust that your unconscious will remember this map.

Corner 1   What is currently happening
Corner 2   What will happen
Corner 3   What will evolve from the previous scene

Corner 4   How all this will change you or the subject of
                your question

QUESTIONS TO KEEP IN MIND

Take special care to include how long in "real-life time" it takes
you to move from one corner to another and try to get names of
people and places at each corner, whether or not you think they
are pertinent to your question. Make a point to note the time
frame in all movements. How long did it take to get from Corner
1 to Corner 2? How long did you stay in each corner? Notice also
whether something is past, present, or future—and then notice
how you notice that.

As you move from corner to corner, new questions will come
up. Notice them. These questions may change with each intuitive
question you start with, or they may remain the same. For example, you may find yourself asking, "Which person or persons are
here?" as you enter Corner 1 (the present). This is simply a broad
orientation question; there are countless others.

If you prefer a still more systematic process, you can ask yourself
a checklist of questions at each corner. Here are some possibilities:

· Where am I?
· Who is with me?
· What is happening around me?
· What am I feeling?

And so on.

The *I* in the preceding questions is simply a metaphor for the
subject of the question. For example, let's say for the "Where am
I?" question I get the sense of my left foot in water. If the subject
is the construction of a building, I might say, "Watch out for the
left side of the building being in or near water."

TWO ILLUSTRATIONS

The following two student readings were done on the first day of
a two-day workshop for people with no prior intuitive training.

As you've done in this book, each student (Mary and Henry, not their real names) was asked to write three important questions he or she wanted to answer during the workshop. And, as you've been doing, they answered their questions many times "blind"; that is, they didn't know which question they were answering while they were answering it.

We'll start with Mary.

Mary's Question

This is the reading of a psychotherapist who recently began pursuing her life's ambition to become a professional fiction writer. Here is the question Mary was reading (remember, she was doing this reading blind): "Will I start seeing clients again?"

Mary's Reading: Gathering Impressions

I divided this workshop exercise into two parts: gathering intuitive impressions and translating them.

Corner 1: This corner is dark, with lots of southern-looking weeds. Neglected. Good things once happened here. There is a hidden pond of magnificent and crystal qualities if you look deeper within. This pond should remain a memory. It should not be reached for in the current situation except in the heart and dreams as memories to create something new. To get to the next corner, I must be willing to walk into the weeds and see the flowers on the hidden side of the vines. I cannot—and should not—walk through the water. I should simply turn and face the weeds. I should allow my imagination to transport me as the terrain changes, and it most surely will.

Corner 2: January or Christmas. Fresh snow and icicles. Carols being sung. I sense opulence and peace here. I get the impression of starting a new family, and a slight sense of a foreign country. A baby is about to be conceived. Everything is safe.

Corner 3: It takes four or five months to get to the next corner, which is summer on Long Island. Working on new projects. Hot, almost hard sun. Jane is riding horses. I am making a decision about a man. I decide to go back, but in a different way. I am at peace after a difficult decision. I see acquiring a house on a hill and being "home."

Corner 4: I am writing for many magazines. I am speaking with educated people. I am in a house in the country. There is another child, two around me, a girl. I am forty-five. I have written two best-sellers. I want to do something different now. I focus on screenwriting. Jane is interested in dance and gymnastics. Maybe the girl will be named Angelica. I see a dark-haired man. He is my friend.

Mary's Reading: Translating Her Impressions

As you know, intuition requires two stages: gathering the intuitive impressions and then translating and making sense of them. With practice, these two stages blend together seamlessly. As with learning anything new, however, it helps to break a process into discrete steps.

Here is Mary's commentary about her impressions:

When I look at these images, I notice that none involves seeing clients. Instead, they are about home and family and creative communication. The first square tells me clearly that I should not go back into the pond (seeing clients) but walk around it, although the way may seem unattractive. My mother is from the South. I wonder if the weeds look southern because I have to work on issues that relate to her. That is also a good metaphor of how I feel about my career change at this time. I didn't expect it to be so tangled and "weedy." In some way seeing clients diverted my energy from my own internal struggles. Writing uses my struggles and the "memory" of the lives of my clients to create something new.

My images tell me that I will want to devote my time to home and family, and that is where my focus will be. I am forewarned that there may be a stormy moment coming up in my marriage, which on some level doesn't surprise me, but I will pay some attention to it in a more conscious way. I feel less pressure to start seeing clients again after this reading, and I have renewed faith that I am going in the right direction professionally. If I had to write this question over again, I would ask if I would have success as a writer, but I guess I answered that one anyway.

Henry's Question

This reading is by a middle-aged manager, Henry, who had recently been fired and had just decided to sue his former employer. Again, he didn't know which of his questions he was answering.

Here is Henry's question: "Will I win the lawsuit against my previous employer?"

Henry's Reading: Gathering Impressions

Corner 1: A blank chalkboard, kind of heavy, the writing beginning to appear in a direction that is not distressing. The pink petal of a rose. I almost want to go to the fourth corner before going to the second. I see two weeks to go to the next corner.

Corner 2: Everything falling into place like so many pieces of mirror or crystal. Bob or rob. I hope the *rob* doesn't mean I get robbed. I see a knob in the center with two hands like the hands of a clock. It takes three months for the hands to come together and another month for them to feel perfect to me. I see my adversary in the center, but not as a threat. The pieces of mirror will cut them if they move in any direction. They must deal with me, and I am the only one who can save them. The next corner comes simultaneously in time but is also my future.

Corner 3: I see California, Silicon Valley. I am working on a big project that feels familiar and new at the same time; like an old idea of mine given a new form. All is well. Everyone wants my time. It's still cool in northern California. A piece of technology I helped design is about to emerge. As it does, the shards in the second corner become falling stars and touch everywhere, wide and brilliant. This may happen before the summer. I learn to enjoy speaking publicly. Money is great. My son is so mature and independent. I don't feel any need to go to the fourth corner because it brings me simply back to the first.

Corner 4: I see a bouquet of flowers, like a bride walking barefoot along a garden path. I see my son at my side and my father with his arms around both of us. I am strong. Karen meets me at the end.

Henry's Reading: Translating His Impressions

I would say that the answer is a strong yes that I will win my suit. The answer addresses my fear that I will have to move for future employment, which is an issue because my wife enjoys her job in Boston, where we currently live. On the other hand, it tells me that I will do well at my new place of employment. Corner 4 reassures me that Karen will join me but also, because of the wording, tells me that there will be some struggle in making this happen. The petal of the rose in Corner 1 and the bouquet at the end tell me that I will win the suit, which has been a moral crusade for me, and that I will simultaneously begin a new life. My mother has been ill and, although I don't want to look at this too much, I am hopeful that, should something happen to her, my father would choose to live near us. My son is only ten months old. It's funny to think of him walking beside me, but I guess that's coming up really soon.

My reading tells me that this suit, which I keep hoping will be resolved tomorrow, will require more time than I had thought. I look forward to reading this again. I feel that there is a great deal more information for me in here.

THE DRAWBACK OF STRUCTURE

Again, moving around a square is simply one way to structure your readings as you get in touch with your own process. You can adopt or invent other procedures. This is a good learning exercise to use as you become comfortable with more "fluid" readings.

Keep in mind, however, that the more you structure your process, the more limited your information becomes. In the coming weeks, try to rely less and less on a rigid approach.

NOW IT'S YOUR TURN

OK, now that you've seen the process demonstrated, I'm going to ask you to do a blind reading of one of your three questions.

≈≈≈

EXERCISE 18
WALKING THE SQUARE

At the bottom of page 128, you'll find the number to one of your three questions. Don't turn to that page until you've responded intuitively to each of the four corners of the square:

Corner 1: The current situation
Corner 2: What will happen in the near future
Corner 3: What will evolve over the long term
Corner 4: How all this will change you or the subject of your question

Now you can consciously forget the corners (your unconscious will remember). Record your impressions, then transcribe them in your intuition notebook under Exercise 18. When you've completed this exercise, you may turn to page 128 to see what question you were reading.

≈≈≈

A PEEK AHEAD

The purpose of this chapter was to introduce you to ways in which you can give structure to your readings. As you gain experience you will undoubtedly develop other methods more suited to your personal style, so feel free to experiment. In the next chapter you will begin to get in touch with the language your intuition uses to "speak" to you.

- 22 -

YOUR INTUITIVE VOCABULARY: WHAT ARE YOUR TIME CUES?

ARE YOU TALKING ABOUT THE PAST, THE PRESENT, OR THE FUTURE?

For obvious reasons, it's important to know whether your intuitive impressions refer to the past, the present, or the future. When we dream, we experience whatever is going on in our dream state as happening in the moment, even if the event might relate to something that has happened in the past or pertain to a time in the future.

Intuition shares this concurrent view of time. Because of this you must provide yourself with markers so that you can frame an event in the appropriate time period. At times these markers will be evident from what you perceive in the answer. For example, you see the person you are asking about as older, or you see events that you know haven't yet happened or even notice something as simple as the progression of a season. If you don't receive such clues, you'll need to see what signs your intuition uses to let you know whether your impressions concern the past, the present, or the future.

My time cues—yours will surely be different—are tangible and unmistakable:

· If my intuitive information deals with the past, I get more "feelings" or "juice" associated with it.

- If my intuitive information deals with the present, I perceive it with a sense of detachment, as if to create distance with which to be objective.
- If my intuitive information deals with the future, it has a light quality, as if I were looking through a sheer curtain. I also notice that I become much less aware of my body, the way one does if a limb goes to sleep, and the information is less tactile and visual and more just a knowing.

The following exercise will get you in touch with your own ways of intuitively telling time and give you a method of focusing your intuition in different time periods by using physical cues.

≈≈≈

EXERCISE 19
ESTABLISHING YOUR PERSONAL TIME CUES

At the bottom of page 130 is the number of one of your three questions.

Sense the question as it is now. Note any impressions. To give yourself a sensory cue for the present, cross your ankles so that your unconscious learns that when you do this, you want to focus on the *present*.

Record your impressions. When you've finished, uncross your ankles.

Put your focus on your left side: your left hand, your left shoulder, the left side of your head, and so on. Curl the toes of your left foot. Note any impressions about the *past* of this question.

Record your impressions. When you've finished, uncurl the toes of your left foot.

Now put your focus on the right side of your body. Curl the toes of your right foot. Note the *future* of this question.

Record your impressions. When you've finished, uncurl the toes of your right foot.

Finally, return to the present to *give advice*. Cross your ankles again to let your unconscious know you are back in the present.

Record your impressions. Remember to use your intuition notebook.

≈≈≈

Two Students' Responses

In the following two examples, I have intentionally omitted the students' syntheses of their readings so that you can draw your own conclusions. Although you are best at interpreting your own symbols and metaphors, a stranger can sometimes read between the lines. Try it.

Response 1

What will my home environment be like a year from now?

The Present: Curtains pulled back on both sides. Elegant velvet curtains. The glass of the window? Looks in instead of permitting the viewer to look out. The curtains have become a shroud of an elderly person who wants to rest but cannot because of grief. This person is hunched over. I lay the person down on a soft cotton-down bed. I see that she is young as I move to the past.

The Past: I get a feeling of activity, anger, and intensity, everything whirling around so fast in self-created motion that there is no time to recharge. I am stifling a scream. When I finally do scream, the old paint and paper on the walls crumbles down around me, revealing a shiny new interior.

The Future: I feel the gentle rocking motion of a lake or stream taking me to greater heights without effort. I get the name James. I see September.

Advice: I feel the need to be organized and to go about my business methodically. If I keep centered, everything will aid me. I should not become trapped by nostalgia and emotion.

Response 2

Will Paul and I work out our differences in a loving way?

The Present: A white plastic arc, like a kitchen ladle, arching to the left. As I continue to look, it gets centered in a semicircle arch, almost like an old-fashioned hat. The hat slices the features of the face away. New features poke through. Hair gets swept up and becomes a drawstring purse.

The Past: The white, bony spine of a person, babe in arms. Weeping at a birth. A burial without a corpse. The baptismal dress becomes a wedding dress, which is used for the next child.

The Future: A solid corporation. An old carved wooden box, an heirloom. One side is full; the other is empty—not, however, from lacking. Rather, it remains empty simply to leave space for future growth (although growth is not needed).

Advice: There are just a few more pieces to come through. Everything is in order. I am laying the foundation. I must not fear change. November. Now. Don't merely watch it happen; try to engage in it.

ONE STUDENT'S COMPLETE READING

The following is how one student did a reading for her sealed question, followed by her interpretation.

The Present: Rocking, a gentle rocking that soothes the situation into balance. The baby keeps wanting to jump out of the cradle. The baby needs to become one with the rocking to achieve its power.

The Past: Drowning; having to breathe in water in order to breathe at all. Learning to accept that the water will not kill. It will not feel good, but it will not damage either. April.

The Future: A souring freedom, summer, but some fear in the freedom of not knowing where it will go. Walking away from what was dear, and finding it is still there in a good way. Two.

Advice: An old book that contains a story waiting to be told. The autumn; I don't want to say the fall. Fear of falling. There is nowhere to fall.

Here's her interpretation once she opened her envelope to see the question: "Will Amy enter college in the fall?"

Amy wanted to take a year off before college, which my husband and I are very much against. Amy doesn't like to focus her energy on anything and prefers to have many interests, which she dabbles in. The images make sense to me in this context.

Regarding the past, Amy has had pressure from us to stay in school for another (hopefully) four years. I don't think that this is easy for her.

Looking now to the future, I hate to say it, but I think that this reading is telling me that Amy is going to do what she wants against our wishes and take the time off.

I don't know what the "two" refers to, but I feel reassured that whatever Amy chooses we will still have a close family: "Walking away from what was dear, and finding it is still there in a good way."

My advice would be that I now think Amy will take the summer off and feel her "freedom" and go to school in the autumn. I think the "fall" is the fear of failure that holds her back from achieving her goals. The book tells me that she will find her path at school. I think that maybe my husband and I should offer her a summer of freedom in return for school in the fall. Maybe we need to put less stress on achievement and more emphasis on her ability to find herself through the variety of things that will be offered in school.

HELPFUL HINT

A reading can be ambiguous. The answer above that the previous student received from her reading was that she would find joy in herself in a new way. The reading also gave her some ideas about where to find the joy and how best to deal with the situation at hand.

In the next exercise, you'll get some practice in the important skill of being able to "follow the thread" of your intuitive impressions.

≈

EXERCISE 20
FOLLOWING YOUR REVERIE

Take the question on page 134 (by now you know not to look until you've completed the exercise). Notice where your attention and perceptions go when I ask you to think about or imagine each of the following things:

- a moment in your childhood
- something that happened recently
- what you'll be doing tomorrow
- a few years in the future
- ten years in the future
- as far into the future as your imagination will take you

Report your impressions. Allow yourself to get detail. For example, if you are remembering a boy named Michael, write the name down. Then notice what he is doing, where he is, with whom, and so on.

Continue in this vein until your reading comes to a natural end. When you've finished, you can turn to page 134 and see which question you were responding to intuitively. Remember to use your intuition notebook.

≈≈≈

ONE STUDENT'S RESPONSE

The following is a reading one student did for his sealed question: *What will I be doing two years from now?*

Singing at a birthday party. The day is for me. My nanny is there. A *C* name.

A frustrating phone call where I felt that nothing was happening. A *J* name.

Eating lunch. My stomach is too full; it's uncomfortable.

Flying in a plane. Going wonderful places.

Lecturing to an audience of intellectuals. I use myself as a good example. Pompous, but happy.

Gardening.

And here is his interpretation when he opened his envelope to see his question:

The birthday party image is easy for me. I give almost all of my time to other people's needs. I want to be numero uno for a while and have someone take care of me. I don't feel like much is happening now. My stomach is too full. I have so many things in the cooker that I am dizzy.

I am trying to get a lot of projects off the ground. Many of these would involve travel, so the "flying in a plane" is reassuring. "Lecturing to intellectuals" is exactly what I would be doing if I take one path I am currently considering. I think this tells me which path would be a good one.

I could be nominated the man least likely to ever garden. Maybe I'll learn to relax. I'm not looking forward to it!

- 23 -

YOUR INTUITIVE VOCABULARY:
ANSWERING YES/NO QUESTIONS

POLARITIES AND YES/NO QUESTIONS

As with your time cues, a basic consideration with most questions is whether the outcome is generally positive or generally negative. I say "generally" because no question should ever be answered simply yes or no. These responses in themselves are too simplistic for a number of reasons:

- Yes or no can change over time.
- Yes or no can be subjective.
- An undesirable outcome can often be changed by changing the present.

In addition to getting a basic yes/no response, then, you should try to get a fix on a question's polarity. A *polarity* is a pair of opposite extremes. Here are some common ones:

- hot/cold
- up/down
- greater/lesser
- heavy/light
- light/dark

Polarities are important in intuitive work. Almost every question can be answered in part or in whole by a polarity such as good/bad, better/worse, sooner/later.

Here are two examples of my polarity associations:

Hot: Active, positive, growing, good, yes
versus
Cold: Rigid, dead, painful, negative
Day: Busy, active, tiring, draining, sometimes positive, sometimes not
versus
Night: Calm, safe, star filled, positive

Of course, my polarity associations will be different from yours. You may find, moreover, that the images you associate with a polarity change over time.

The following exercise will give you a chance to get in touch with your intuitive polarity associations.

≈≈≈

EXERCISE 21
ESTABLISHING YOUR POLARITIES

Focus. Get a sense of each of the following polarities. Record your intuitive impressions of each.

- hot/cold
- day/night
- high/low
- heavy/light
- good/evil
- helpful/harmful
- nourishing/depleting
- growing/shrinking
- smooth/rough
- clear/entangled
- developing/eroding
- rising/falling
- birthing/dying
- forward/backward
- beginning/end
- high/low

Doing this will help you establish what symbols your intuition uses to alert you to positive or negative aspects about a question. Remember to use your intuition notebook.

≋

Now that you've begun to recognize your polarities, the next exercise will give you a chance to see them in the context of an actual reading.

≋

EXERCISE 22
GETTING POLARITIES IN YOUR READINGS

Now you'll answer a series of five questions (listed at the bottom of page 138) with a yes or no.

Notice your first response in handling each one. Do you feel yes or no? How strong is that feeling? If you sit with the question, does that feeling change? If so, why? Take each question into the future, perceiving how far in the future you are, get another polarity, and describe it.

When you've finished recording your impressions—remember, you'll need to get polarities for all five questions—turn to page 138 to see which ones you were responding to. Remember to record your responses in your intuition notebook under Exercise 22.

≋

SOME STUDENT RESPONSES

To give you an idea of the kinds of polarities students report, here are four examples:

- Will Henry be my only child?
   Hot. Stalemate. Up (like a reversed arc). Heavy changing to light, not dense. Future is a nonquestion.

- Will I get a promotion in September?
   No (yelled). I put my foot down. Yellow. January. Dust.

· Will I sell my house at my asking price or better?
   Yes. Singing. Spring. Light, but full of energy. Empty, but a
   positive empty. April. Cash.

· Will Steven propose to me?
   Down. No, for now. February. Yes.

HELPFUL HINTS

If you got conflicting answers, your intuition may have addressed
conflicting parts of the same question. Sometimes an initial no
answer has yes imagery. **When in doubt, trust the imagery and
not the yes or no.**

DEVELOPING POLARITY SYMBOLS

To use polarities as a tool, you must first notice what symbol system you already use to define polarities. You must also create new
symbols to use for nuances and checks.

The word *hard,* for example, can mean "concrete" as well as
"difficult." To decide which, you must determine the qualities of
hard in each specific reading:

· What other polarity symbol does hard lead you to?
· Is it a positive or negative symbol?
· What are its qualities?
· Do the polarities change over time?
· How do the polarities change over time?

These questions will make more sense as you become increasingly acquainted with your intuitive process.

Response to **Exercise 22:** The first question was your Question 2. The second question was
your Question 1. The third question was your Question 3. The fourth question was your
Question 3. The fifth question was your Question 1.

DEVELOPING NUANCES

There is even nuance to something as simple as the yes/no dichot-omy. It's especially important to second-check a yes/no answer because these answers don't come in the form of symbolic puzzles, which help the brain to analyze and pick up substantiating detail. In more involved reading processes, we deduce an affirmative or negative answer from the complex information we pick up. This information helps us understand why a given result occurs. With yes/no answers, we reverse this process and get the answer first, then substantiate it. You'll find that sometimes in doing this, the answer *changes*.

Example 1

Consider the question *Is Martex a good investment?*

> No. Down. Hits floor in two months. Yes, growing green for two weeks. Hits floor again—no.

From this reading you know that Martex is not a good invest-ment at the moment because it's going down over the next two months. It then recovers for two weeks before bottoming again.

Example 2

Will I get the job I interviewed for on Tuesday?

> No. Smooth, slippery. Ten days. Hard. Definitive, positive. Yes, in a week and a half.

Example 3

Will my new series be a hit?

> A beautiful dark blue container. I don't know if it's a bottle that needs a top or a vase. The container was formed by a pool of tears that took form and became useful. The vase now has flowers, and it's still early in the season for flowers. The flowers are a Valentine's

gift but aren't stable until April, when the vase can grow its own. A small, green semicircle of glass attaching to the blue vase and sheltering its base. October, new life growing already for two months, beach and working. Take a long breath and allow the vase to exist without making it a container.

I'll translate the last reading line by line in conversational language.

I don't know if this series is a onetime chance or a continuing opportunity. My perception that this is my "only chance" comes from my history and the grief that I haven't completely worked out. The grief has given me useful talents. Being in this series helps transform my pain from something limiting into something that enables me to be creative. I need to be able to do that on my own, and I will be able to by April. Something new will come up in August, and I will feel good about doing it by October. I need to work on trusting the process without feeling that each opportunity is my last chance and thereby limiting myself.

My conclusion is that the series will not be a bust nor will it be a hit. If it concerns my participation in this series, it will be transitory. I will get another job by the end of the summer. It will add a new color or dimension to my work.

By the way, this is also a model for giving a "professional" reading, which you'll soon learn to do.

- 24 -
DEVELOPING YOUR INTUITIVE READING STYLE

LET'S JUMP RIGHT IN

In this chapter we'll be expanding the ways you access and interpret your intuitive information. Let's start with an exercise.

≈

EXERCISE 23
GETTING A SENSE OF YOUR INTUITIVE STYLE

By this stage, you're probably aware through which sense you receive most of your intuitive data. Are you predominantly visual or auditory? Do you "feel" your information or do you receive it by imagining changes in the environment around you?

Answer for yourself the following questions:

- What symbols or images do I receive in a reading that always mean the same thing?
- What is my preferred sense?
- What is my most frequent "interference style"?
- How do I remedy my interference?
- What sense do I trust the least?
- Does my preferred style change when the time changes: past, present, or future?

This is not a reading, so you can record your answers directly in your intuition notebook.

≈

HERE ARE MY RESPONSES

Noticing your reading style will help you better understand and place the information you receive in a reading. These are important questions to ask yourself frequently. Your reading style will change as you practice intuition and in response to changes in you or different conditions in your life.

For example, when I have a head cold I tend to use feeling as opposed to seeing (which is usually my preferred intuitive sense). A sun is always indicative of a positive outcome in my intuitive vocabulary. The sense I trust the least is feeling. As a result, I always try to use another sense to verify it, such as by asking, "Does what I'm seeing agree with what I'm feeling?"

My most frequent interference style is doubt, which I remedy by taking a deep breath and noticing the first thing that comes to mind in a general sense before refocusing on the specifics of a question.

GETTING IN TOUCH WITH YOUR INTUITION
IS A PROCESS OF SELF-DISCOVERY

The ways you tap your intuition will undoubtedly be very different from the ways I do. It's important that you develop your own process. Your intuitive style is a reflection of your unique personality just as much as your intuitive vocabulary is. And keep in mind that your intuitive style can evolve as you get in touch with this latent ability.

About the only way to discover your intuitive style is through trial and error. As you practice using your intuition, you'll discover certain talents and habits, preferences and rituals that are more conducive than others. To take a simple example, you may learn that you work better in the morning rather than at the end

PRACTICAL INTUITION   143

of the day. You may find that you're more effective with your eyes closed than open. You may discover that you prefer questions written on paper or read aloud.

As noted earlier, intuitive information can arrive in three primary ways: seeing, hearing, and feeling. No one of these is any better than the others, and most people use a combination of all three (although one usually predominates). What's more, your intuitive impressions may be very accurate with one sense (say, sight) while less so with another.

Intuitive styles can express themselves in highly idiosyncratic ways. You may be quite accurate picking up names but a washout at dates. Much of this depends on how you "direct" your intuition. If you have melancholic tendencies, your intuition will be focused in the past. A paranoiac, on the other hand, will be riveted on the future.

Where does your attention habitually go? That is usually a good indicator of where your intuition will focus. The intuitive who is excellent at assessing the future may have difficulty reading the past or present.

INTUITIVE AIDS AND TECHNIQUES

Some intuitives find that they work better using techniques such as the *I Ching,* tarot cards, astrology, or even tea leaves. These methods can put a framework on otherwise disorganized information. They aren't, however, the most efficient ways of getting a good individual framework, because each of us has that inside ourselves, and, with patience, we can develop it.

Additionally, one must be very careful with things like cards because often with them there are even odds that instead of interpreting what is going on, you'll interpret what you hope or fear is going on. More intricate styles, like the *I Ching,* are better because in them you have, in a sense, more uncontrolled steps. The more random a technique is, the more likely it is to work.

The key difference between intuition and these other divining techniques is that with intuition you're not using external cues to help you—or to lead you astray.

Doing Formal Readings for Yourself or Your Friends

Pulling It All Together

We've already covered most of what you need to do a formal reading for yourself or others. In this chapter we'll clean up loose ends.

As with everything else in this book, don't think you must memorize all I say. Again: It's important that you realize I have intentionally made a natural process (that is, intuition) more difficult so that you become conscious of what you already do unconsciously.

Remember, you are already intuitive.

Before You Begin, Let Your Subject Know How You Work

You need to let your subject know your intuitive style before you begin so the reading will go smoothly. Here are some points you should be sure to make:

- **You don't need "helpful" information other than the question.** The *less* you know about the topic, the better your intuition is able to respond.
- **You aren't always right.** Intuitive information is always valid, but the interpretation can be off the mark.
- **Your subject still needs to exercise judgment—and his or her own intuition.** You're giving your friend infor-

mation that will be *helpful* in reaching decisions. You aren't making those decisions for your friend!

· **You're not a therapist.** It's easy for friends to become "reading junkies," bringing all their problems to you. If a friend comes to you more than a few times a year (business readings aside), she or he is becoming too dependent.

In addition, you'll need to let your subject know other aspects of your intuitive style, for example, whether you prefer the questions written down on slips of paper, asked out loud, or merely thought.

Before I give a reading to another person, I issue my standard warning, which goes something like this:

> I'm going to do an intuitive reading. Some of my information will be correct, and some will not. My batting average is pretty good, but if anything I say feels wrong to you, it probably is. You know your own information, intuitive and otherwise, better than anybody else. Don't give that power away to me. You're here to get a *different* perspective—not the "right" perspective.
>
> Anyone who tells you she knows more about you than you know yourself, or who tells you he is 100 percent accurate, is someone to be very wary of.

HAVE YOUR SUBJECT PREPARE QUESTIONS BEFOREHAND

In addition to the points just listed, have your subject compose the questions before he or she sits for a reading. You'll also have to explain briefly the importance of framing questions carefully.

Having your subject prepare questions serves two functions. First, he or she does a "prereading" by the selection of questions and areas of interest. Second, this preliminary work gives your unconscious a prepared field of questions. I often answer all of a client's questions just by having him or her ask the first one, because my intuitive information then leads me to the other areas of concern.

As you well know, however, your friend's questions will raise yet other questions, and before you know it you could veer off into many areas of the questioner's life. Use these "detours" as part of the reading, but tell your friend that he or she should feel free to get you back on track if the digression does not seem helpful.

GETTING RELAXED AND CENTERED

Once you've introduced yourself to your subject and told him or her how you work, you'll need to get to your intuitive state.

Find a comfortable seated position and begin to relax. Take a long, deep breath and exhale slowly, allowing your conscious mind to take a rest. As you continue to breathe deeply, let yourself become aware of the physical sensation of being in your body—your bones, your internal organs, your skin and muscle, the beating of your heart.

Start to notice your body relaxing and your mind quieting. You don't have to "clear your mind" before you begin. Take all the "garbage" in your head as part of the reading.

Continue this step for a few minutes. When you feel calm and centered, you're ready to begin your reading.

ONCE THE QUESTION IS ASKED, BEGIN SPEAKING AS SOON AS POSSIBLE

As I mentioned earlier, the longer you wait for information, the more opportunity you give your reasoning mind to butt into the intuitive process.

You may get impressions even before a question is asked. Record those too. Your intuition knows what question is being asked before the question is completely verbalized.

You may get impressions seemingly unrelated to the question. Your intuition may respond to a question about sounds, for instance, with smells.

Report everything. Impressions that may have no meaning for you may be highly revealing to your friend.

DON'T LET YOUR SUBJECT INTERRUPT YOU

As you begin speaking, your subject will often be tempted to interrupt you, with either a confirming "That's right! That's right!" or a contradictory shaking of the head.

Remind your friend that such interruptions interfere with the intuitive flow, and that when you need feedback you'll ask for it. Keep speaking until the intuitive impressions taper off. Your subconscious will let you know when your intuition has answered the question.

IF YOU DRAW A BLANK

Sometimes you'll be asked a question and not "get anything." First, don't assume you aren't receiving valuable intuitive data. Assume that whatever you're picking up is in response to the question.

But if you really aren't receiving any tangible impressions, try looking at the same scene from different perspectives. If you can't see, for example, whether you'll get the job you've applied for, examine the prospective employer instead of yourself, or examine your best friend's reaction when you tell him or her the news, or ask whether you'll be moving to the city to accept the job.

Don't be afraid to say, "I'm not getting anything." You can articulate your process. For example, if a friend asks you whether she'll move to Los Angeles and you don't receive any impressions, you might say, "I'm not getting anything. Now, I don't know if that's because I'm really just not picking up anything or because I don't see you in Los Angeles."

TRANSLATE YOUR IMAGES

Although giving your original perceptions—such as "I see a tree in a yard full of poppies"—may at times be helpful, try to give as much information as you can in a conversational tone as you do in the interpretation stage.

Let's say your subject asks you about a new project and you get a sense of a balloon becoming too large and bursting, you might report that things are expanding too rapidly and unsustainably. Then you might add some of your imagery, which might be more literal to the questioner than you realize. For all you know, the project involves balloons!

You will find that the more you practice your intuitive skills, the easier it will be to do all the sensing and interpreting work internally until you do it almost without noticing anything but the interpretation while keeping the original information close enough to your consciousness that you can refer to it for clarity.

≈≈≈

EXERCISE 24
AN APPLE A DAY REVISITED

Do you remember the apple exercise we used to predict the movement of the gold market (Exercise 12 on page 70)? The same technique can be used on just about any question you can think of. Take the time to record descriptive details such as where the apple is, who it belongs to, whether it gets eaten, and so on. You're using the apple as a metaphoric framework with which to examine any object.

Here we'll use the first apple to represent the present, and the second to represent the outcome or future. On page 150, you will find which one of your questions this exercise refers to. Without turning to see what it is, use your intuition to answer it.

Record your reading under Exercise 24 in your intuition notebook.

≈≈≈

ONE STUDENT'S RESPONSE

Here is the reading and interpretation one student did of her question "Will I have children with John?" Like you, she did not know what her question was until she opened all her envelopes at the end of the seminar.

A little hard green apple. A little misshapen, but cute. It might be from an old crab apple tree that I have in my backyard. It tastes better than I thought.

The second is a tiny crab apple. It's not good to eat on its own, but it makes a wonderful jelly. You have to gather lots of them. They belong in groups; I see three.

Now let's see how she interpreted her reading once she learned which question it referred to:

John certainly is a little hard green apple. He's not too sure he's ready to have a family, but it looks like we will. We will be happier together because of it.

This is a good exercise for a "quick hit" on a question you'd like answered. Don't let the apple restrict you; you can use the fruit or object of your choice.

REPORTING YOUR IMPRESSIONS

Once you begin receiving impressions from your subject's question, additional questions will arise. Try to go from the details to the big picture. As we discussed, you want to try to look at the situation from different perspectives.

Don't forget to look for *verifiable* signposts. You want to give yourself and your subject checks and balances to help assess the accuracy of your interpretation.

AT THE VERY LEAST, MAKE SURE YOU LOOK FOR THESE THINGS

Every question is different, but on your initial round of impressions, you should look for the following data:

- Do you get a good or bad, positive or negative feeling from the question? Try to get a *polarity*—yes or no—for the question.
- Where is your attention placed *in time*? When you hold this question, do you feel like you're in the past, the

present, or the future? If you move your attention ahead
into the future or back into the past, does your impression of the question change?
· Do you sense any *people* or outside *events* affecting the
question? Any names? Any initials?

Again, make sure to look for any other signposts or "markers"—names, dates, places, history—that your subject can either
prove or disprove. This lets both of you know whether your intuition is on track.

OTHER USEFUL QUESTIONS

The following questions will stimulate anyone's intuition. They
can be adapted for your personal or professional use.

· What are the qualities I admire in this person?
· What are the qualities most people admire in this person?
· What things could this person teach me about?
· What words does this person need to hear to have a hap-
pier life?
· What would be a good challenge for this person to work on?
· What problem or challenge has this person recently over-
come?
· What good change will happen for this person in the com-
ing year?
· Which people are or will be difficult in this person's life?
· What is a common mistaken assumption made about this
person?
· If this person were an animal, which animal would he or
she be and why?

And so on. You will undoubtedly think of variations in your own
line of work.

WORKING WITH FEEDBACK

While you should not ask for information or clues about a question initially, at certain points you may need to ask your subject to clarify the question or to help you make sense of your impressions.

HOW DO YOU REMAIN OBJECTIVE—ESPECIALLY WHEN YOU PICK UP DISTURBING INFORMATION?

The eternal challenge facing the intuitive is maintaining objectivity in the face of questions that are highly charged for the person asking them. Remember that people ask intuitives for help because they have major questions or issues to resolve.

Let's say, for example, your friend asks you whether she will marry her fiancé. Or whether she will land the big promotion she has been hoping for. Now let's say you get nos to these questions. How do you inform your friend of news you know will be hard to take?

The most important thing for you to realize is that **you can't assume any event is necessarily good or bad.** Perhaps not marrying the fiancé or losing the promotion is a blessing in disguise.

At other times, however, you'll have to break hard news to a friend where the blessing is difficult if not impossible to discern. Naturally you'll want to be as gentle and tactful as you can. If possible, present the information in metaphor that can be loosely interpreted and let your friend assemble it. Also, instruct your intuitive sense to give the silver lining, so you can present that. Finally, remind your friend that you can be wrong.

Feel free to edit information you think is harmful or unethical to reveal (such as medical information if you aren't a doctor). And, most important, feel free not to answer a question.

Don't ask your subject to verify information. The information given in an intuitive reading done for another may be private. Often the subject understands the reading better than you do because it's about his or her life. That's as it should be.

I remember in a workshop in California one of my students, Janet, walked over to me very upset. She had been giving a reading to another student, Lydia, and began to intuit unspeakably violent incidents from Lydia's childhood. If what she was intuiting was correct, she had the good sense to know that by giving this information she could upset Lydia and make her feel invaded or exposed. If she were incorrect, the information could also be damaging.

I told Janet to "forget" the information itself and instead ask herself intuitively what Lydia needed to extract from this information. Without actually specifying any information she had received, Janet turned to Lydia and, in the most casual way, said, "Nothing that happened to you when you were young was your fault."

Lydia began to cry. She revealed to Janet that she had been horribly abused by her parents and been forced to do things that she knew, even at the time, were not right. Lydia wanted to know more from Janet, but I intervened, saying that it is important to know when an intuitive is not helpful, and that a psychotherapist was the appropriate person with whom to uncover and process such information.

≈

INTUITION IN ACTION
A STUDENT'S ANECDOTE

My whole family has asthma. One day my son had a bad asthma attack at school. He was sent to the hospital and kept there for days. During this time, I kept feeling that his lungs were irritated and that it might not be asthma that was causing his condition. I mentioned this to the doctor, who insisted on his diagnosis. I called a friend who had also trained in intuition and asked her to look at my son's lungs, and she received the same information. I asked for a second medical opinion, and the diagnosis of asthma was confirmed.

A month later my son was still having difficulties, and I told him that I couldn't shake the feeling that it wasn't asthma. He looked at me like I was a witch and then confessed that he had inhaled a spray of Mace, thinking that it was his asthma inhaler, and he had been afraid to tell me because he thought I would be angry with him.

≈

THERE IS NO SUCH THING AS A FALSE HOPE

Hope in and of itself is valuable. One can have hope and still confront a situation honestly and deal with it realistically.

Once you are in the interpretation stage of intuition, your knowledge, emotions, biases can all find a way into your process. It's important to notice what you think and feel separate from what you intuit when your answer is unclear. The remedy to the confusion often lies in a conflict between these perceptive modes. People's own intuition about themselves and their environment is usually more accurate than your intuition about them (although it may not be as clearly defined).

If you want an outcome and your intuition says no, ask why.

Intuition sometimes misses its target, and then logic and empirical observation come into play. One time I was living in Rome, and a child with chronic eczema was brought to me. I looked at this child, who had a simple skin problem, and thought, "Of course she'll heal." The girl lived in my neighborhood, so I could see her frequently; after three healings she still made no response.

I knew that outbreaks of eczema are often stress related, so I searched intuitively for emotional stresses. I felt that some tension between the parents and an older relative was causing the girl to be anxious and making the eczema worse, and I mentioned this to the mother. The mother told me that her mother-in-law had recently moved in with them, and the family then made a special effort to deal more consciously with the stress this was causing. The child's eczema, however, still did not improve.

Finally, I resorted to reason. I suggested to the mother that she, together with the child's physician, insist on getting the child into any experimental program available for the treatment of eczema.

She called her doctor who, after some investigation, said that there had been some success in an in-patient program in which children were given very limited diets and tested for food allergies. The child was having so many ill effects from her disease and the social rejection it provoked that her family decided to put her in the program, which required a monthlong hospital stay (anyone with children knows they can't be trusted to stay on a diet). As you probably guessed, food allergies were discovered, and today this child remains symptom free (except when she breaks her diet).

Logic won the day. My foreknowledge of this particular disease process (which may or may not have been accurate) had finally guided my intuition in only one direction, blocking out other useful information. It took some clear thinking to find the answer.

OTHER ETHICAL CONSIDERATIONS

Before treating patients a physician goes to school for many years and takes an oath to heal. A psychotherapist knows the workings of the psyche and how to guide a client to healing. An intuitive simply gets information. Make it a rule never to mimic a trained and licensed professional in a given field.

I have often guided people to go to their doctors for an examination when I sensed a problem. And I have asked people to investigate a certain time in their lives with their therapists. I've learned through my own mistakes that it is not always helpful or ethical to reveal information, even when it's correct!

A READING WITH TRAINING WHEELS

One approach some of my students find helpful is not to know the question the subject is asking. Clients can assure this by writing the question down on a slip of paper and handing it to you folded over, or by thinking the question. Even though you don't see the question at first with this technique, having it written down is helpful because this forces your subject to frame the question carefully.

DOING READINGS FOR GROUPS

I rarely work in front of groups. The kind of personal information received in an intuitive reading is best given in private. The two exceptions are when I work with a company and a group of people need to hear the information in order to act on it effectively, and when I teach, where the students need to see examples in order to improve their technique.

Many if not all of the exercises in this book can be used with a group to brainstorm questions. If the entire group is practiced in intuition, you can simply verbally propose the question. If the group is new to intuition, it's better to do the reading blind, by putting the questions in envelopes (one for each participant) without revealing the questions, then stepping the participants through the process.

Have each member of the group make his or her contributions before brainstorming and suggest that the intuitive dialogue continue during the brainstorming process. This process adapts well to strategic decision making for both families and businesses.

A FUN GROUP EXERCISE

When you're with your family or a group of friends, have everyone write his or her name on a piece of paper and place it in an envelope. Make sure both the envelopes and the pieces of paper the names are written on are all the same.

Mix up the envelopes and then distribute them facedown so that nobody knows who he or she is reading. A greater understanding of the issues or dynamics of a situation can be acquired in this way, as well as empathy for each point of view. It's especially insightful when people get their own names!

When I do this exercise in workshops, I repeat the process as many times as there are participants, so each participant gets to do a reading on all the envelopes. This is also a useful conflict resolution technique.

A MEMORY OF INTUITIVE COLLABORATION

Medical research is often a step into the unknown. Drug toxicities, adverse reactions, tolerable yet useful dosages are not known at the beginning of a drug development trial.

Approximately eighteen months ago I began consulting Laura Day, a well-known psychic or intuitive, concerning research ongoing or planned at my Sutter Street medical offices. I not only asked about the drugs to be researched, I also asked about the ways the research was being conducted.

Laura's most important contribution to date has been her input in the PEG-Interleukin II trial. Laura accurately predicted the side effects of flu-like symptoms and local skin irritation. When we were advancing the doses, she warned of neurological side effects. Within that month, one of the volunteers suffered a stroke. We introduced a lower intermediate dosing step into our trial and proved that dose safe to administer.

In another instance I asked Laura about a compound called NAC (N-acetyl cysteine). She accurately predicted that it would cause abdominal pains in some patients. She felt it would be a useful drug to fight HIV disease. Trials to prove its usefulness are being conducted both at Stanford University and at the National Institutes of Health.

Throughout the trials on Trichosanthin, a drug that kills infected macrophages and infected T-cells, Laura was supportive that this drug would prove useful in the treatment of HIV disease. Now, two years into the trials, we are showing that this drug is indeed killing the HIV virus, and excitement in the research community is building.

These are but a few of the instances where Laura's advice has cautioned to move more slowly or reassured me to keep going though the early results didn't look as promising as had been hoped.

(Excerpted from a letter written November 23, 1991, by Dr. Larry Waites)

≈≈

- 26 -
USING INTUITION TO IMPROVE YOUR DECISION MAKING

INTUITION SHOULD ADD TO GOOD JUDGMENT, NOT REPLACE IT

I'm sure that, by now, you are more in touch with your intuitive process. Never forget, however, that you shouldn't use intuition as the sole guide in your life, any more than you should allow logic to be the sole guide.

A dangerous misconception about intuition is that it should be used to make decisions. The best use of intuition is not to decide whether you should do something but simply to add information to what you already know and feel. Intuitive information should not be considered in isolation, but then neither should emotional or sensory or logical data.

Identifying how our intuitive faculty works enables us to use it selectively for effective decision making. A predominantly linear process may be preferable when clear, empirical information is available. When little data is at hand or the question relates to how current choices might affect future results, an intuitive process may be more efficient.

It's helpful to learn techniques by which intuitive data can be clearly separated from intellectual and emotional data.

FOR MAXIMUM EFFECTIVENESS, USE YOUR INTUITION SELECTIVELY

Modern psychology has moved in the direction of integration. But when using your intuition, you want to keep the various inputs—your senses, your knowledge and judgment, your feelings, and your intuition—*separate.*

If your intuition tells you to do a certain thing that your feelings also tell you is the right course of action, and then in investigation of the facts your judgment confirms that it looks like a solid move, you can be assured of a good outcome. Instead of getting lost or merged, intuitive data can be matched against what your senses tell you and what your thinking tells you and what your feelings tell you, giving you a powerful system of checks and balances.

What we need to do, then, is force our reasoning mind to take a backseat. In many of the exercises so far, I deprived your mind of empirical data. Without information to analyze logically or emotionally, you were forced to rely on your intuition.

INTUITION PLAYS A PART IN ALL YOUR DECISION MAKING

Even though you may be unaware of the process, every decision you make to some degree uses your intuition, as well your knowledge, your judgment, and your feelings. Even when making a decision such as "Should I go to Florida in February?" you use what you know about Florida as a vacation place, how you feel about going to Florida, and mixed in there—often as "the reason you couldn't put your finger on"—what you intuit the trip will be like.

At the risk of oversimplifying complex psychological processes, you evaluate situations based on four sources of information:

- what you *know* about them (your knowledge and memories)
- what you *think* of them (your judgments and interpretations)
- how you *feel* about them (your feelings and emotions)
- what you *intuit* about them (your intuition)

Is any type of data more valid than any other? No, but emotional data is the least valid. I believe in feelings rather than emotions, though in our society we pay a lot of attention to emotions.

Feelings are emotional senses without explanation. We tend to dismiss feelings as subjective, but in their realm, feelings are facts. If you feel angry, it's an objective fact that you are feeling angry.

INTUITIVE INFORMATION IS EASILY LOST, SO LEARN TO RECOGNIZE IT

One reason you haven't been more aware of how intuition contributes to your decisions is that it's easily dismissed as feeling. It's also highly likely that you override the counsel of your intuition with your logic. In other words, the stream of intuitive data you are constantly receiving is drowned out by the information provided by your senses, emotions, memories, and intellect. This is especially true during moments of confusion.

With the practice and feedback this book has provided, you've begun to learn how to distinguish among your knowledge, your feelings, and your intuition. Being able to extract the intuitive aspect from the mélange of your decision-making process will give you the ability to use the information gained in this manner as substantiated fact instead of a blind hunch.

When using this method to contribute to a decision, write what you know about the problem or choice, what the logical decision would be, what the decision would be if you followed your emotional needs, and then your intuitive perceptions. This creates a solid portfolio of information with which to make your choice.

The point is to keep your intuition separate from your knowledge and feelings initially, so that it can later be integrated to greater effect. It's not as simple as that, however. You must make sense of that information—and act on it. Intuitive information is always objectively valid, and it is always right. It's in the interpretation of intuitive data that errors are introduced. To lessen the chances of this, intuitive data should initially be kept separate from logical or emotional data, so that these different modes can complement one another.

What is unique about intuition, as opposed to logic or our other decision-making processes, is that with it we can as easily—

if not more easily—get information about the future, or about things that don't follow a pattern. Sometimes logic or hope will challenge your intuitive "hit" about a situation. Since intuition involves interpretation, you need to investigate further, especially when your intuition, knowledge, emotions, and faith don't all agree on a course of action.

Now it's time to see how this process works with your three questions.

First, for each question write down what you feel the answer is.

Next, for each question write down what logic and your intellect tell you the answer is. Justify your answer.

We will be comparing your thoughts and feelings with your intuitions in Chapter 29.

- 27 -

USING INTUITION IN YOUR PROFESSIONAL LIFE

MORE LOOSE ENDS

You now know more than enough about the operation of your intuition to use it successfully in both your personal and your professional life. In this chapter we'll look at techniques that are especially pertinent to business and finance.

I have worked as a consultant with many kinds of groups: businesses, medical practices, film productions, therapy and healing groups, venture capital groups, and families. Lots of exercises and practices target the questions and needs of each group. There is a different practice for restructuring a company than for reworking a creative project, but the premise is the same: You just need to ask the right questions. I'll give a simple practice to use both in groups of family and friends, and in business for strategy and problem solving.

Whatever your expertise—psychotherapy, mechanics, home-making, medicine, writing, painting, engineering—you are the one who best knows which questions to ask in your field. Ask your intuition the same questions that you would ask your intellect and its body of knowledge. The difference is that when you ask questions of your intuition, you can ignore the limits of time, and space, and experience.

It's often helpful to write down the list of questions you use in your work. Some professionals, like physicians and stock analysts, have a set of standard questions (your intuition will give you new ones). When you are working on a creative project, the square exercise (on page 127) is often very helpful because it gives you an end result that you can work back from.

When you work in an intuitive group on the same question, often the readings are very different but not conflicting. Each person looks for the data from the point of view of what he or she deems important. The troubleshooter will look for problems, while the cheerleader will look for what is working. Some people tend to get the patterns in the question as a whole, and some see the fragments that are inconsistent or especially important. There are as many reading styles as there are kinds of people. Their readings may appear to vary, but that's because each is intuiting different but equally accurate parts of the question.

Nonagreement is very constructive in readings because it promotes deeper examination of the material. Intuitive information is so rich and complex there is always more information to be gathered from one reading. This is extremely useful in getting a comprehensive grasp on the question and the varied options for action toward resolution.

READING PEOPLE IN THE COURSE OF BUSINESS

The following exercise illustrates a powerful technique for reading and understanding other people. As you will see, it is especially useful for any professionals—including doctors, therapists, negotiators, lawyers, teachers, and social workers—who need deep insight into other people.

≈≈≈

EXERCISE 25
TRADING PLACES

Pretend that you are someone else, a person who is integral to the answer of the question listed at the bottom of page 164. You don't have to know all about the person you are embodying before you begin. The person you are pretending to be may even change as the exercise progresses.

Take a long, deep breath. As you exhale, allow the person you are embodying to name him- or herself. The following are questions for you to answer as the person you have chosen to be for this exercise. You don't need to memorize this list; I provide it to give you an idea of the *types* of questions you should ask.

- Describe yourself in detail.
- What is the major focus in your life right now?
- In what ways will your focus change over the next few months?
- How do you feel about the world around you?
- What do you need?
- Are you on the right track?

As you "get into" the reading, how do your initial impressions of this person compare with your final ones?

Record your impressions under Exercise 25 in your intuition notebook.

≈≈≈

This trading places technique lends itself easily to variations. Modify the questions by listing the ones *you* would want answered in order to better work with a client. If you use this technique to answer a question and you feel the answer does not describe a person related to it, use the description as a *metaphor.*

≈≈≈

INTUITION IN YOUR PROFESSIONAL LIFE
EXAMPLE 1

You are a physician "working up" a new patient. You peruse the patient's history and note gastrointestinal disorders. The patient's complaints are the same as they have always been. All prior tests for ulcers and other "suspects" have been negative. She has responded well to small doses of a barbiturate-based elixir with her old doctor.

Before you prescribe the routine medicine, the idea that your patient may be pregnant crosses your mind. You have no reason to suspect pregnancy, but you direct your nurse to run a blood test. Your patient looks at you as if you were nuts.

Your patient tests positive—and it's a good thing you checked, because the prescription she was going to be taking can cause complications in pregnant women.

EXAMPLE 2

Everyone in your investment club is talking about a hot new stock. Indeed, in the last few weeks your broker has called you several times to recommend it. You request an annual report, and the audited numbers are better than you expected. Despite a price run-up during the recent buying frenzy, you believe there is still a great deal of upside left in the stock.

Every day you make a mental note to call your broker to purchase 1,000 shares. With one thing or another, however, you always seem to forget.

Lucky for you. At the end of the week, the stock crashes. A competitor has arrived on the scene with a lower price point, an analyst has changed his rating from "outperform" to "underperform," and mutual funds are tripping over themselves to dump their holdings.

Thank heaven you didn't buy that stock—and, while you're at it, thank your intuition.

≈≈≈

- 28 -

USING INTUITION IN YOUR PERSONAL LIFE

HOW I USE INTUITION IN MY LIFE

I thought that the best way to illustrate how you can use intuition in your personal life would be to take two examples from my life.

The most dramatic example involved a trip I was planning to Rome back in the days when I commuted frequently between New York and Italy. I had carefully planned my trip to be in Rome for as many days as I could while still keeping two engagements I had in New York, one at each end of the travel time. At the last moment I felt uncomfortable about leaving New York in what, at that instant, felt to be a rush.

So the day before I was to leave, I decided to delay my trip for a day at significant cost. I was on the plane two days later when the news reached me: My flight would arrive late owing to delays at the Rome airport. The reason? There had been a wild shooting with many casualties—at precisely the time I was originally scheduled to land!

Would I have been shot had I remained on my original flight? I can't say for sure, but it's not something I would have wanted to test my luck on. Still, my intuition was strong enough that I was willing to delay my trip at great expense.

This is not something to do on a regular basis. For example, I have often traveled to Los Angeles during periods many psychics have predicted that California would sink into the Pacific Ocean and Nevada would become beachfront property. I look for myself. If I don't get any information that tells me to change my departure or arrival dates, I don't. I have experienced a few tremors but haven't yet had to test my swimming skills.

I remember a reading I did for myself a decade ago while I was in Italy. I intuited that my apartment in New York had been robbed. I got the song "Oh! Susanna" playing in the background. I saw my friend, who was supposed to be looking after the apartment, not paying attention. I made a mental note to ask him about his big stomach, even though he was quite thin. I'd also had a dream the night before that my cat's tail was bent.

I called to check on the apartment, and my friend told me that he had sent his friend Susie by to water the plants and feed the cat because they had just found out that his girlfriend was pregnant and they were in shock. I asked him if Susie, who I did not know, had been by my place yet, and he told me that he had just left the keys for her that morning. I told him to get the keys and give them to my friend Paola. Then I called Paola to tell her to change the locks. A week later she called to let me know that she had taken my cat to the vet because his tail had gotten stuck in a door and it now had a big bandage on it.

Although I do not know if all the elements of my intuitive journey to my home were correct, I think that it was judicious to avoid having Susie enter my apartment considering the accuracy of the other "hits."

A reading and a dream told me many things.

Intuition as an integral or daily practice can enrich your life in a variety of ways. I like to do an intuitive exercise every morning. The question is often vague, like "How am I?" or "What should I know to better live this day?" Sometimes I prepare a variety of questions at the beginning of the week, put them in envelopes, and answer them blind. I always prepare fourteen questions for a week so I won't know even in the final days what I'm answering. I also often put the same question in more than one envelope.

You can do this daily practice with a friend or your spouse by swapping envelopes at the beginning of the week and doing a reading on each other's questions each day. This can give you a sense of your day, your life, and yourself and in so doing keep you centered in what truly matters to you. It also helps you avoid a great deal of irritation. I have finally learned that if I look at a picture and think, "That could fall," it means I should move my bones and fix it before it does. There is nothing more frustrating than saying I was right after some unwanted event has happened.

THE CIRCLE TECHNIQUE

In Chapter 21, I introduced you to a technique called Walking the Square. In it I used a square as a framework with which to view the progression of events to reach a particular outcome. In the Circle Technique, you view a question by giving details concerning the different internal and external influences affecting the situation.

If you need a tangible image to work with, draw a circle.

· You are the center of the circle.
· Your external influences and environment lie outside the circumference of the circle.
· The circle's circumference itself is the contact boundary between you and your external influences.
· Shake the circle up to merge the perspectives for a possible outcome or an overview of the situation. What does the inside of the circle look like now? What does the outside look like? What does the contact boundary look like?

≈≈≈

EXERCISE 26
THE CIRCLE TECHNIQUE

You will be responding to the question listed for this exercise at the bottom of page 170.

Now, imagine that you are in the center of a circle. Allow yourself to receive an image to describe yourself. What is that image?

Allow an environment to grow around you in your imagination. Describe what it is like in the center of your circle. Then look out and describe what is around you.

Imagine now that you are the circumference of the circle. Describe yourself.

Imagine that you can perceive outside your circle. Describe the environment. Who or what do you find there?

Imagine you are standing outside your circle looking in. What does the circle look like from this perspective?

Record your responses in your intuition notebook under Exercise 26. When you are done, you may turn to page 170 to see which question you were reading.

≈≈≈

ONE STUDENT'S RESPONSE

Here's the reading one student did of the question in her sealed envelope with this technique:

> *The Center of the Circle (You):* Blue velvet; the nap does not know which direction to travel. The fabric is fragile, easily ruined and not as easily repaired. There is fear in this but also depth. Beneath the fabric is calm. I want to travel down and transform the interior so the fabric is not needed at all. Inside, all is in order.
>
> *The Outside of the Circle (Your Environment and External Influences):* The outside of the circle is pushing in. I am trying to figure out which question this is; I get an *M* name that is hostile. The outside is fighting with itself over the circle but not really touching it. The circle is pressured by the sense of external conflict. Now I see a rip in the circle and something black trying to get in and darken the blue velvet. I see January, maybe January 11. I see the black circling the blue but not engulfing it. The blue gets denser, and the black dissipates above it. I see spring flowers. The blue relaxes out to fill the circle again, although it is still a denser color at the center. I want to ask myself when the blue will be uniform again. I see it turning to a lovely purple in August, not losing the growth of the spring but transforming it into something more appropriate to the season. The purple leads to an altar in September, or maybe early October, because I see pumpkins but not jack-o'-lanterns yet.

The Circumference (What Is Between You and the External Influences): I get a difficult feeling, the hard outside is meeting a yielding center, and wherever the center yields the outside can push the circumference until it rips. I don't want to harden the circumference; I want to increase the density and resolution of what is inside until it supports the circumference so much that the line delineating the circumference becomes unnecessary. As I say this I realize how difficult that is. I search for an alternative. I think that the alternative is to make the circumference so dazzling that it blinds the intruders. I look for how this can be achieved. It can be achieved by remaining calm. I get the name Jody or another *J* name.

Shaking It Up (Merging the Information to Obtain an Outcome): I see a spent volcano. I see an *A* month—April. I see the mountains and a new place, see traveling around the volcano, which is now dead and will never erupt again. The volcano really died in the spring, but I didn't get my fire back until now. The fatal blow came on January 8. The exterior of the circle is no longer an issue. The circumference and the center are one. I am in a different circle altogether.

Here's how she interpreted her reading once she opened her envelope to see her question: "Will the conditions at my job improve?"

You could knock me over with a feather! If I believe this reading, it seems that I will leave my job! That has been a private fantasy of mine, but I vacillate a great deal, which is a problem in other parts of my life as well. The first part is an accurate description of what it feels like to be me. I like what I do, but there are too many conflicting personalities in my work environment. I know exactly who the *M* person is.

I have a difficult time holding my own on the job because of my habitual indecision. I never really pick a course of action and stick to it, so it is easy for others to "push me around." I think there is some advice here in my impressions about finding a way to hold my ground.

I think this reading tells me that things will improve on my job by spring, but I will leave the job around August anyway. It looks

like I may even be fired. I get a sense of many spots occurring
sometime in January, early January. It doesn't look like I can do
very much to change the situation, except perhaps protect myself
with greater decisiveness and resolve.

If I don't have a new job in August (the purple center), I will
certainly have one by the fall (the altar). If I were not at this job, I
would consider moving back to Hawaii, where I grew up. I moved
to California in my twenties, never intending to stay for long, yet
I have been here now for over a decade.

HELPFUL HINT

You can do this exercise in reverse by looking at the future ("shaking up the circle") first and then asking what the different elements of the circle require for a positive outcome.

- 29 -

A FINAL LOOK AT YOUR THREE
QUESTIONS

GET YOUR NOTEBOOK AND TRANSCRIPTS READY

Begin by organizing your readings with their respective questions.
If you haven't recorded your interpretation or "translation" of any
of the readings, do so before continuing. Take each reading as a
complete answer and try not to let your other answers to the same
question influence your interpretation of each reading at this
point. When you have completed this task you can begin to integrate all of your responses into an "answer." Let us begin.

Take both your original information and your interpretations
for Question 1. Consider the following questions:

· Do all your readings agree? If they don't, does the disagree-
  ment illuminate other options?
· Do your answers address the question directly or do they
  address other areas of your life more?
· In which ways are the untranslated readings similar?
  Which names, time periods, places, feelings, and so on
  agree?
· In which ways do your readings agree with or differ from
  your emotional or intellectual assessment of the question?
· Now use the answers to these questions and any other
  questions that come to you to build a comprehensive
  answer. Then put the answer in a conversational tone,
  as if you were giving it to a stranger who didn't believe

in intuition. You've had practice doing this in your interpretations of the individual readings you have done.
  · Look at the ways your readings differ, if they do, and use the differences as a reading about the choices you have in dealing with the question.

Repeat these considerations for your other two questions.

Once you evaluate your answer, you need to ask yourself which other questions the answer elicits and then look for those answers in your original material. Now take all the information you have. With the readings that involved past, present, and future, organize your information in consistent time sequences (past impressions together, present impressions together, future impressions together).

Let's take some time to interpret your information as a whole. If some of the information conflicts, is there any information in your readings or in what you know about the situation that could explain the discrepancy?

If you don't like the result, is there any information available in your readings about how to change the result? During which time period and by what action would change be appropriate?

TYING IT ALL TOGETHER

Having completed all the exercises in this book, you now have a great deal of information about your questions. Gather your notes, putting your collections of answers with each of your questions. Consider the following questions regarding your readings:

  · What do all your readings on a particular question have in common?
  · What do they tell you about the outcome of your question?
  · Do they give you any perspectives on your question?
  · What new questions do they bring up about your original question?

You will probably notice that your responses to each question gave you a lot of additional information, unrelated to your question, about your life and how it is changing. You can use the completeness of this information to make better choices. Look at all the information that you received to find options instead of answers.

- 30 -

Random Speculations Regarding Intuition, the Nature of Reality, and the State of Our World

Some Parting Thoughts

My aim in this book has been to help you rediscover a forgotten ability and to hone it into a useful tool. My aim, in short, has been practical.

Nonetheless, as we began to discuss in Chapter 10, the existence of intuition has some profound implications for our worldview. I don't know how intuition works, but the fact that it does work tells us something about existence and life.

I would like to leave you now with some notions you can mull over in the coming weeks and months.

Why We Have Intuition: A "Scientific" Hypothesis

Like your other senses, your intuition is first and foremost a survival tool. It's geared to give you data instantaneously. When our day-to-day survival was more precarious, an individual's life or death depended very much on how tuned in he or she was to the surrounding environment. Those who were most intuitive had a far better chance to survive.

We tend to rely on our more "advanced" and "civilized" senses, but remember that our most reliable senses are the ones that developed first. Our sense of touch develops before our sight, our intellect last of all. Nature tells us what we can count on to survive—and we were given intuition for a reason.

Most of your life questions relate in some way to the future, and intuition, being foremost a survival skill, is especially adept at addressing the future. Most likely it's the sense (or collection of senses) specifically geared to gathering information that is not available in your immediate environment.

For most of us, this process takes place unconsciously and with much interference from our logical minds and emotional patterning. In becoming aware of our intuitive information before it's fully assembled and before we have unwittingly acted on it, we bring this valuable data above our emotional consciousness to the level of our intellect. As a result, we make better reasoned decisions. It's in separating this intuitive information from our feeling and thinking, which may or may not be correct in their assumptions, that intuition becomes a useful tool for us.

THOUGHTS ON COMMUNITY

The body is a community of cells and physical experiences, the mind of thoughts and memories, the emotions of experiences and reactions to those experiences; and a single human being is the composite of all these things working effectively or not in community.

Our relationships are a community of human beings who belong to many different communities: work, social, family, political, ideological.

Let's take a moment to look at our communities. We've relegated our physical, spiritual, and emotional bodies to doctors, psychiatrists, and churches or political/ideological organizations. We go to channelers to ask the angel Gabriel what we already know and could see if we would look within ourselves to where the answers lay. We do all of this at great cost and often outside of or at the most distant parameters of our community.

I'm not saying that all these professionals and institutions don't have a place and provide a service, but we use these services while not even knowing our neighbors.

When I first moved to my little neighborhood in Rome, what lured me to the "ghetto," although I could not have named it at the time, was the fact that, if your lights wouldn't go on, you called a friend who had an uncle who was an electrician. If you felt ill, you called your neighbor first and your doctor second.

The use of intuition and healing, the recognition that we are all capable, and the discovery that indeed there are no experts give some power back to individuals over the care, use, and maintenance of their lives, from the cells in their bodies to the solidity of their relationships.

If I had one message to share with you in this book, it would not be "You are intuitive." It would be **We are all more capable of giving help than we realize.** And, for that matter, your neighbor has more to offer you than you might think. Give help and ask for help, and in doing so bless your community with sharing.

ABOUT PREDESTINATION

A common question, even among experienced intuitives, is "If I can predict events, does that mean that everything is predestined and fated?"

If you could convince me that all events and actions were predestined, I would never do another intuitive reading. I would simply live life. There is much that lies outside our field of influence (such as the time an earthquake will occur, and where), but there is much that lies within it—we don't have to be at the epicenter on that day.

The practice of intuition is enlarging our field of influence, experience, and possibilities. If you can identify a future event and/or identify the series of conditions that create it, you can choose to cocreate a different future if it lies within your field of influence, or choose a different response or action if it doesn't. You have already done that by doing the exercises in this book.

Making a prediction is viewing the strongest possibility. Predictions tend to be accurate because the pattern of any system, including human beings, tends toward stasis. I often hear people tell stories of predictions that scared them, such as "She said I will have a car accident in July."

I would have asked the following questions *as a starter:*

· When in July?
· In what color car?
· Who's driving?
· How serious is the accident?
· Who is with me?

And I would most certainly not forget the most obvious question: How can I avoid this event?

ABOUT THE COLLECTIVE CREATION OF REALITY

Imagination is the passageway to the resources of our mind and experience. Imagination is the ability to create and embellish, and what do we create from but our memory and experience and the information available from the collective unconscious and what I would like to term the collective conscious?

The collective conscious works on the belief that our actions—individually, and collectively as a planet and a system—create a pattern and direction that, unless intercepted and rerouted, is determined by the motion of the past and present.

Think of a ball. You roll the ball, and it goes in the direction you roll it, and, if you know the terrain it's rolling over (the obstacles it will encounter) and the speed at which it started, you can make a fair guess about where it will end up.

Now think of thousands of balls rolling in all directions. If you know where all the balls started from, then you'll know at what speed and at which point your ball will meet another ball and change direction. You will also have information available to allow you to alter the direction of a ball. In fact you'll have the resources to alter the direction of all the balls that your ball comes into contact with, directly or indirectly, by altering just one ball.

Reality is nothing more than a consensus.

ABOUT THE INTERCONNECTEDNESS OF THINGS

If there is anything intuition demonstrates, it's the interconnect-edness of everything. If you believe in anything Carl Jung said about synchronicity, everything is connected on some level. All that's missing is a question—the right question. Psychic ability has nothing to do with one's religious or spiritual beliefs, although the kind of openness that intuitive training engenders can be use-ful in finding guidance along our spiritual paths.

The fast development in technology over the last half century is slowly being joined with a set of ethics concerning its use so that the wonderful advances we have made don't destroy us and our planet. The "building" has grown too tall, and we are, somewhat reluc-tantly, returning to its base to strengthen the foundation. This will bring up questions about how we want to use our technological and natural resources, in what ways we want to develop further, and how to safeguard what is of greatest value to us. We are having to search our spirits for answers to our material choices. The material and the spiritual are seeking harmony with each other.

Communications, travel, and trade are such that we are ever more going to be part of a heterogeneous world community. Ideally, this will encourage us to look for ways in which we are connected and illuminate the part of us that transcends race, nationality, religion, political system, and ideology.

No two snowflakes are alike, but their ability to lay together in a communality creates a snowfall. It's through our intuition that we can explore not only our differences but our oneness. This search for connectedness—whether to our planet, to God, or to one another—is my definition of spirituality.

ABOUT SHARING SPACE ON THIS PLANET

Through our intuition we can explore not only our differences but our oneness. In this book you have allowed yourself to "know" events, people, and perspectives beyond your field of direct experience, and they have affected you and your path. What does that say about the impact on the world of how you practice being you?

We have begun, as a society, a practice of ecology. We have at the same time allowed our practices of social ecology to erode. We often fail to honor the people in our environment as we should, and we don't often enough reach out to one another with kindness. I try to remember how important it is to smile at people on the subway, even though I live in New York City and I'm rational enough to be aware that I shouldn't smile at everybody!

I try to teach my son to say good morning and good evening and really mean it. I give my seat to the elderly (even though lately I'm forgetting my own age and decrepitude and giving my seat to someone near my age, raising eyebrows). When you realize the amount of information and feeling and vision you are able to intuit from others, doesn't it lend credence to the wisdom of "Do unto others," since we certainly share our experiences, both good and bad, in some unconscious way?

The practice of intuition is an important part of this system. By adding intuition back into our formula, we can reclaim some of the decision-making power we have delegated to educated strangers. By sharing our intuition with one another, we can provide valuable resources that are beyond our field of knowledge as well as the awareness that we are intimately affected by one another's experiences.

ABOUT SPACE AND TIME

If everything is interconnected, then we must seriously revise our current notions of space and time. Intuition teaches us that things are separated neither in space nor in time. There is no past or present or future. We make these distinctions because as human beings we must be able to give some kind of structure to the world—otherwise we would all miss our appointments!

People today feel a need to reconnect with those things that cannot be measured, things that transcend and give meaning to life. Yet intuition is still largely distrusted. It's disconcerting that we live in a culture that so values the contributions of logic and intellect that we ignore a vital part of ourselves.

ABOUT SPIRITUALITY

We can use our intuition to gain greater clarity about our sense of the spiritual world. Just as the emotional lens through which we perceive ourselves and our environment is different for each person, our individual senses of spirit are unique to each of us. Even if every person claimed to believe in the same God, if all were asked to describe their sense of God and faith, each description would be different. It's the depth that individual interpretations of faith offer that evolves our communal beliefs to create greater depth for all of us.

-31-

Free Bonus: How to Turn Anyone into Your Own Personal Psychic in Five Minutes!

Say Good-bye Forever to 900 Psychic Hotlines!

It's impossible to watch late-night television without encountering one infomercial or another promoting "psychic hotlines." Half the former stars of prime-time television have been rescued from oblivion by pitching their own "genuine, tested" psychics. Judging from the variety and frequency of these shows, these stars have been doing quite well for themselves.

The appeal of such expensive guidance is natural. We live at a turbulent time in an increasingly complex world, and many people yearn for guidance.

I won't comment on the accuracy of these psychics on call twenty-four hours a day, but I promise you one thing they *won't* tell you is that *anyone* can do what they do—with little or no training.

At this point you might ask, "Why did I read this whole book and work so hard on the exercises if *anyone* can do an intuitive reading with five minutes of preparation?"

That's a fair question. While anyone can generate intuitive information, it takes an experienced practitioner to interpret the information in a useful way. The skill is in knowing how to ask questions, and how to interpret the intuitive responses.

Another Person Can Be Helpful

Why, you might be asking, do you need another person's intuitive impressions when this whole book has been about training you to do this for yourself? The answer, in short: to get an unbiased reading. It isn't easy to be objective about our own lives. As you'll see shortly, enlisting a friend and providing subtle guidance as he or she "flies blind" gives you a source of pure intuitive impressions. Again, your task will be to make sense of those impressions.

By the way, you don't have to limit yourself to one reader. There is no reason you can't invite a number of your friends to give their intuitive impressions, thereby allowing you to form a consensus of intuitive hits. These brainstorming sessions can be fun, as you'll see shortly.

ANYONE CAN BE YOUR OWN FREE PSYCHIC HOTLINE

Remember the two parts to a reading: receiving intuitive impressions in response to a carefully worded question and then translating and interpreting those impressions. A novice can generate accurate—and objective—intuitive information for you with very little preparation if *you* ask the questions and interpret the answers.

How do you get people to give specific and accurate intuitive information? You have to fool them—as I did you in the opening chapters of this book—because most people do not believe they can answer questions they haven't seen.

Here's how you do it.

Step One: Setting Up a Double-Blind Experiment

A double-blind experiment is used to ensure that the researchers' expectations do not bias the results. To evaluate a new drug, for example, a double-blind study would mean that neither the patients nor those administering the study knew whether any given subject was receiving the actual drug or a placebo.

This exercise is my version of the double-blind experiment. In it you will provide answers to questions that neither you nor the person asking them knows!

Write a number of questions on separate but identical sheets of paper. When you have finished, fold each one in half, then in quarters. To emphasize that these questions are sealed from you as well as your reader, you can place each sheet in a separate envelope.

Step Two: Explaining the Ground Rules

Tell your readers that you are about to offer them each a sealed envelope that contains a question, and you would like them to report whatever impressions they get in response. *Do not tell your readers that they are doing a reading, or even that they are answering your sealed questions.* Doing so will very likely raise their internal resistance to intuition. One approach that often works is to tell your intended readers that you are conducting an experiment, and that you need their participation. All you ask is that they follow your instructions. Here is a speech I typically use to "initiate" a reader:

> As you know, I have sealed a number of questions in envelopes. In a moment I will give you the first. I would like you simply to report all your impressions about the question you will hold in your hand.
>
> I know this will feel strange to do. You won't know what the question is, nor will I. I don't expect you to "be right." Simply trust that anything you say in response to the question will provide me with valuable information.
>
> Before I give you the envelope, take a deep breath and notice what you are aware of internally as well as in your external environment. Notice how you feel right now. What are you aware of through your senses of sight and hearing and smell? What thoughts or memories or images are going through your mind? This is a "baseline" check of your awareness so you'll recognize how your perceptions change once you hold the envelope.
>
> In a moment I'll hand you the first envelope. I am going to ask you to report everything you imagine, every memory that comes to mind, everything you see, hear, feel, or think. In short, I want you to report *all* your impressions—even if they don't make sense or seem silly or made up.
>
> OK then, let's start. Take a few deep breaths. I am going to hand you the envelope now. Please start speaking immediately and continuously. Remember, if you get stuck and nothing comes to you, make something up.

Adopt a playful attitude of mock seriousness. Remember, you want to help your readers *pretend* they can answer the sealed questions.

Step Three: Recording Your Readers' Responses

When you have finished with your instructions, hand your readers each an envelope, note the number, and get ready to take down the impressions they report. You may find it helpful to use a tape recorder rather than attempt to transcribe everything your readers say. **Although you will very likely realize which question is being responded to, do not open any of the envelopes until all have been read.**

Helping Your Readers Through Interrogation

Since your friends don't know the questions they are reading, they cannot use logic to "figure out" the answer. By telling them to make up a response if necessary, you firmly close the door to their reasoning process and force them to rely solely on intuition. The resistance of even the most stubborn reader is overcome with the suggestion that he or she pretend to know the answer to the sealed question.

If your readers are sincerely stuck and tell you they are not getting anything, tell them to pretend *that* is part of the answer! Another thing you can do if your readers get stuck, or go in a direction you don't understand, is ask them to elaborate each response. Since you don't know which question is in each envelope, let your intuition guide you.

Here are some useful questions to guide your readers:

- Do you get a yes or a no? What makes you think so?
- What sense do you get regarding this question six months from now? A year?
- What names come to mind? Do you get any initials? Describe them in detail. What are they doing?
- Which places come to mind? Describe them in detail.
- Which memory comes to mind? Describe it in detail.
- What feelings come to mind? Describe them in detail.

Don't tell your friends the questions before you have had a chance to look at and evaluate their intuitive impressions. If your "personal psychics" are vague, ask them to elaborate. This may take some active questioning on your part.

Here is a dialogue I recorded with someone I used as my psychic:

LAURA:	When you saw Jerry, what was he doing?
READER:	I don't know, I just saw my friend Jerry.
LAURA:	Look at Jerry again and tell me about him.
READER:	I really haven't heard from him in a long time, but I know that he was going through a career change when we last spoke.
LAURA:	Do you think the change was successful?
READER:	I don't know; I haven't heard from him.
LAURA:	What's your guess?
READER:	I guess he was on the right track, but it would take a little longer than he anticipated.
LAURA:	How much longer?
READER:	How should I know?
LAURA:	Guess. Give me the first number that comes to mind.
READER:	OK, three. Are you happy?
LAURA:	Three what? Days? Weeks? Months? Years?
READER:	Shorter than years, longer than weeks. Months, I guess.

And so on. We continued this "interrogation" for some time. As you can see, you may have to cajole your readers!

Step Four: Interpreting and Evaluating Your Readers' Impressions

A novice will normally respond using language that you understand because his or her unconscious will already know that you are the interpreter. Your readers' impressions will usually make more sense to you than they do to the readers.

You will find that much of what a novice makes up is accurate. Why? It's easier for the subconscious to respond to your question than to search for something to make up. Once the process has begun, your friend cannot help but read.

Open the first envelope and look at the question. Now that you have documented your friends' intuitive impressions, apply your reasoning abilities to interpret their relevance to the question.

Compare what your emotional or rational mind says about the question with what your intuitive mind does. If the question was "Will I get a promotion at work within the next six months?" your intuitive response may be different from your logical response. Comparing and combining these different modes of sensing creates a solid portfolio of information with which to answer the question.

It's perfectly acceptable at this point for your friend to help you interpret his or her intuitive images and impressions. Let's say that your friend kept picking up the letters *B* and *L* while reading your first envelope. Without your friend's feedback, you may not realize that these are the initials of her former employer and represent your former employer in her reading for you.

HOW TO BE YOUR OWN PSYCHIC

If you are having trouble being objective in reading your own questions, you can go through this procedure by yourself. Write the questions on separate sheets of paper, number them, and then key your readings to the numbers. You'll undoubtedly be curious to see how you did, but wait until you've finished reading all the questions before opening any of the envelopes.

A PLAYFUL ILLUSTRATION

To demonstrate how accurate a reading rank beginners in intuition can give, I played the following game with three skeptical friends. We had just finished dinner, over which I told them I could train anyone to be a psychic in five minutes. Since we were in a mood to rent a movie that evening, I proposed the following challenge: One of us would select a film at random from a thick movie guide; the other three would describe it in detail *before* the selection was made!

As with the sealed envelope technique I just described, this would be a truly double-blind experiment. The three readings we are about to analyze were done simultaneously on notepads to prevent anyone from being influenced by another's reading.

The first two (Beginner A and Beginner B) were complete skeptics about intuition, so I told them to pretend they were psychic. I gave them a modified version of the speech I presented earlier in this chapter, and we began.

Information that seemed tentative or doubtful from the inflection of the student's voice, or even my own, is indicated with question marks. You will note that my reading was more concise than that of either student. As you gain experience, you'll need to do less groping for words with which to express your impressions.

Beginner A's Impressions

Horseback riding. Cowboys? Smoke. Beach, sand. Perhaps hot and dry like the West, but at the edge of mountains. I get a sense of crossing a river, a lake, or some other body of water to find someone or escape. Eighteen hundreds to early 1900s. American West. Desert. Hot and dry, perhaps Colorado. Someone trying to get someone else. Action takes place outdoors, not a Woody Allen–type intellectual film. Mostly men involved. Not really a love story. A search for something or someone, a chase. Robbery, money involved? *Butch Cassidy and the Sundance Kid?*

Beginner B's Impressions

Dinosaurs loping across a field, like in *Jurassic Park*. Jelly beans shaking in a jar. Splashing in the water, like the Gene Kelly scene in *Singin' in the Rain*. *The Holy Grail*. A sentence typed repetitively, like Jack Nicholson in that horror movie *The Shining*. Trash that I smelled when I left my apartment this morning. Lollipop. Swimming rapidly in cold water, maybe away from a shark or a whale, or even a dinosaur like in *Jurassic Park*. Escaping and wetness, raw. The thought that I'm not very good at this sort of thing. The feeling that I'd like to be more trusting and intuitive, and wondering what I'm supposed to be doing. An island. Innocent people trying to live their lives. Small-town America. Nineteen sixties, 1970s. I'm sorry, but I'm fixated on *Jurassic Park* and *Jaws*.

My Impressions

Country. Flowers. Sound of music. Woods, long ago. Long dresses. No indoor plumbing, but technology nearby. The making of a family or the building of a team or project of the community (to save an animal). I get the name Sarah. Prairie, prairie days, 1800s. Diverse people or concerns coming together. Building a windmill, healing a family or community.

When we'd all finished writing down our impressions, our other friend closed her eyes, opened the movie guide, and pointed at a movie.

The Envelope, Please

She selected *The Matchmaker* and read the capsule description. The original cast included Shirley MacLaine, Paul Ford, Anthony Perkins, Shirley Booth, and Robert Morse. Based on the play by Thorton Wilder, this comedy is about a middle-aged widower who has decided to find a young bride. The matchmaker he consults has her eyes set on this prosperous if stingy businessman, while the ingenue he wants falls in love with one of his clerks.

You may recognize the more popular musical version as *Hello, Dolly!* Its cast included Barbra Streisand, Walter Matthau, Louis Armstrong, Michael Crawford, and Tommy Tune.

How'd We Do?

To see how closely our readings compared with the actual movie, we went out to the corner video store, rented the movie, and watched it. All three of us picked up a sense of a small town. Not bad.

Two of us felt, correctly, that the movie was set about a century ago. Beginner B felt that the movie had something to do with the sixties. He was also not too far off the mark: The movie was made in 1958, while its musical version, *Hello, Dolly!* premiered in 1969.

Two of us picked up a sense of a small-town America, set in the West or prairie in the latter part of the last century or the early part of this one. Although the movie takes place in Yonkers and New York City in 1884, the film's setting reminds one very much of a small frontier town, with horses and unpaved streets in a time just before automobiles and skyscrapers. Again, not bad.

I picked up the name Sarah. There is no character in the movie named Sarah. But when I learned what the movie was about, I realized that Sarah is my younger sister, who at the time was planning her wedding! Remember that the movie concerns getting married.

I picked up that it was a love story about building a family. Even more fascinating, however, is that both students, who are single men, felt the movie involved a chase or danger of some kind.

All in all, our readings were quite accurate, especially since we had absolutely no clues to go on. I'm sure that as a group we could easily have selected *The Matchmaker* from a list of a hundred possible films with little difficulty.

WE INTERPRET "TRUTH" AND "MEANING" THROUGH THE SCOPE OF OUR EXPERIENCE

The impressions each person received reflected his or her unconscious psychology, often in highly revealing ways. It's interesting, for example, that Beginner A, a middle-aged bachelor, got such a strong impression that the movie was "not really a love story." In a sense, he was correct. The movie is a comedy that includes mistaken identity and individuals pursuing others under false pretenses.

Beginner B, on the other hand, is a middle-aged gay male. He viewed the predatory qualities of the matchmaker in the movie in terms of escaping from sharks, whales, or dinosaurs (the match-maker, incidentally, was hardly svelte). Beginner B probably learned more about himself during this reading than he could had he been in weeks of therapy.

As a philosophical point, there is no truth or "out there" to be divined. The meaning and significance of intuitive impressions as well as of your everyday impressions reflect your unique individuality.

- 32 -
YOU'VE ONLY JUST BEGUN YOUR JOURNEY

THE START OF YOUR INTUITIVE APPRENTICESHIP

Naturally, I'm a strong believer in the intuitive process, but this makes my process even more empirical than most people's. I know that the supporting information for any decision is available if I use all the resources at my disposal: intuitive, emotional, intellectual, empirical, and experiential. If I cannot find the facts to support an assumption using these means, I know it's faulty.

There are fewer things to learn than we realize. Much of life is uncovering what we already know and experiencing both the power of each new tool and the ability to build another piece of what we dream once we have the tool in hand.

I apologize for having presumed to teach you something you already know. I'm sure you'll enjoy using your newfound skill to create more of what you want in your life and to help those you know create more in theirs.